Scales

Formulas and Uses

ABOUT THE AUTHOR

Jody Fisher has worked professionally in virtually all styles of music during his career, from straight ahead and contemporary jazz to rock 'n' roll, country, pop and show groups. He taught Guitar and Jazz Studies at the University of Redlands in Southern California and at the Idyllwild School of Music and the Arts (ISOMATA). An active performer in the Southern California area, he still maintains a private teaching practice, serves on the faculty of the University of La Verne, and as an associate director of the National Guitar Summer Workshop's California and Nashville campuses. Jody Fisher is also the author of the *Guitar Mode Encyclopedia* and the National Guitar Workshop's jazz method series, *Beginning*, *Intermediate*, *Mastering Improvisation* and *Mastering Chord/Melody Jazz Guitar*, also published by the National Guitar Workshop and Alfred.

Guitar Chord & Scale Finder

A Handbook for the Improvising Guitarist

JODY FISHER

ISBN-10: 0-7390-2529-5 (Book)
ISBN-13: 978-0-7390-2529-1 (Book)

Acquisition, editorial, music typesetting and internal design: Nathaniel Gunod, Workshop Arts
Cover photos: Jeff Oshiro

TABLE OF CONTENTS

Chords

INTRODUCTION

The purpose of this book is to give you a single source to refer to when looking for information regarding the use of scales for improvisation. This is not a method. Rather, it is a reference book. Use it in the same way you would an encyclopedia.

The sections are arranged by chord type (major, minor, etc.) which are all shown with C as the root. Four voicings of each chord are shown. A quick-reference *Chord and Scale Chart* will allow you to easily find out what scale goes with each chord, depending on the chord's *function* (see page 8 for a thorough discussion of *chord function*). The Chord and Scale Chart is followed by the scales that can be used for improvisation. Scale construction is covered in standard notation with a brief explanation about how to use the scale. Finally, two fingerings are illustrated in diagram form.

Since all chords are shown with C as their root, it will be very important for you to transpose these fingerings into all the different keys. The chord and scale fingerings in this book are "moveable," that is, they contain no open strings and therefore may be moved around the fingerboard freely.

While the use of scales in improvisation is important, it is only one of the many subjects you must study to become a proficient improvisor. Melodic patterns, arpeggios, composition, technique and harmony are but a few of the other topics you should consider looking into. For a detailed study of scales and modes, see my *Guitar Mode Encyclopedia*, available at stores everywhere. Practicing the use of all the scales is also very important, and there are many products on the market today that will help, such as the *Stand Alone* series published by Alfred and the National Guitar Workshop.

Have fun and enjoy the sounds!

HOW TO USE THIS BOOK

Reading Scale and Chord Diagrams, Scale Formulas and Roman Numerals

SCALES

This book is loaded with scale diagrams. The top line represents the first string of the guitar, and the bottom line the sixth. The vertical lines represent frets, which are numbered with Roman numerals.

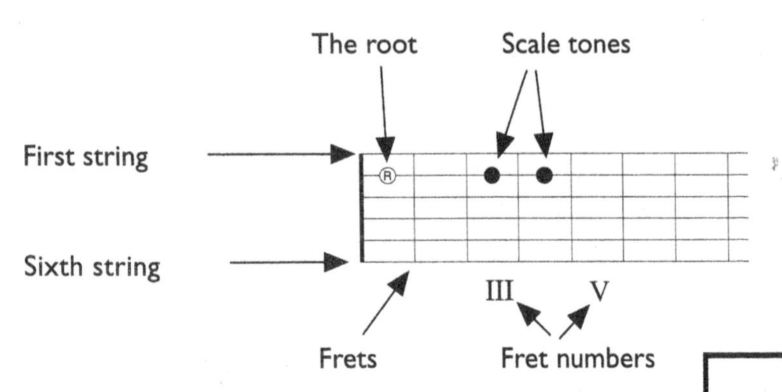

SCALE FORMULAS

Each scale in this book is shown in standard notation with its formula in whole steps and half steps.

W and ⁄\ = Whole
H and ⌒ = Half

Here is an example showing a C Major scale and its formula.

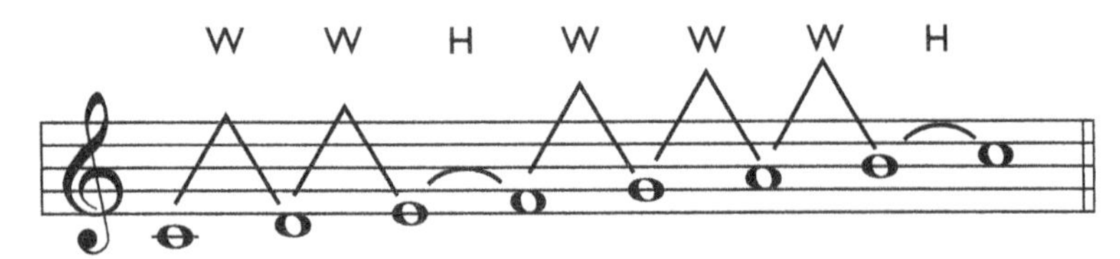

CHORDS

There are two to four voicings given for every chord type in this book, so there are lots of chord diagrams to read. They are similar to the scale diagrams, except they are oriented vertically instead of horizontally. Vertical lines represent strings, and horizontal lines represent frets. Roman numerals are used to number the frets.

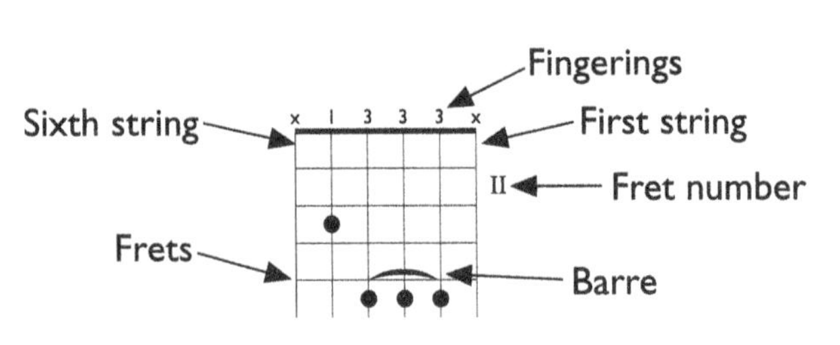

ROMAN NUMERALS

Here is a review of Roman Numerals, in uppercase and lowercase, and their Arabic equivalents.

I	i	1	IV	iv	4	VII	vii	7	X	x	10	XIII	xiii	13	XVI	xvi	16
II	ii	2	V	v	5	VIII	viii	8	XI	xi	11	XIV	xiv	14	XVII	xvii	17
III	iii	3	VI	vi	6	IX	ix	9	XII	xii	12	XV	xv	15			

Reading the Chord and Scale Charts

Every section in this book includes a Chord and Scale Chart. Use this chart to learn what scale(s) will work over the chord in question. To make proper use of the chart, you will have to determine what key the tune is in, or the key of the specific part of the tune you are working with (see *Determining the Key* below). This will then help you determine the exact function of the chord you want to improvise over. As soon as you know the key of the tune and the function of the chord, the Chord and Scale Chart will help you learn what scale(s) to use.

Here is how the charts look:

Chord and Scale Chart

Chord	Function	Major or Minor key	Scale or Mode	Starting on...
min9	ii or vi	Major	Minor Pentatonic	The root of the chord
	ii	Major	Dorian	The root of the chord

This chart explains that if the tune is in a major key, and a min9 chord is functioning as ii or vi in the key, you can improvise with a minor pentatonic scale built up from the root of the chord. You will also notice that the chart says you can use the Dorian mode starting on the root of the min9 chord if it is functioning as ii in the key. Sometimes the chart may indicate that a scale should start on a note other than the root. For instance, it may indicate that a scale can be used "starting on" the 4th of a chord. Just figure up a 4th from the root of the chord, and use the resulting note as the root of the indicated scale. For instance, a 4th up from the root of a C chord would be F.

Determining the Key

The overall key a song is written in can be determined by looking at the key signature which is located between the clef and the time signature. Every key signature has a corresponding major and minor scale. Since each scale contains a different number of sharps or flats, you can easily figure out what key the song is in.

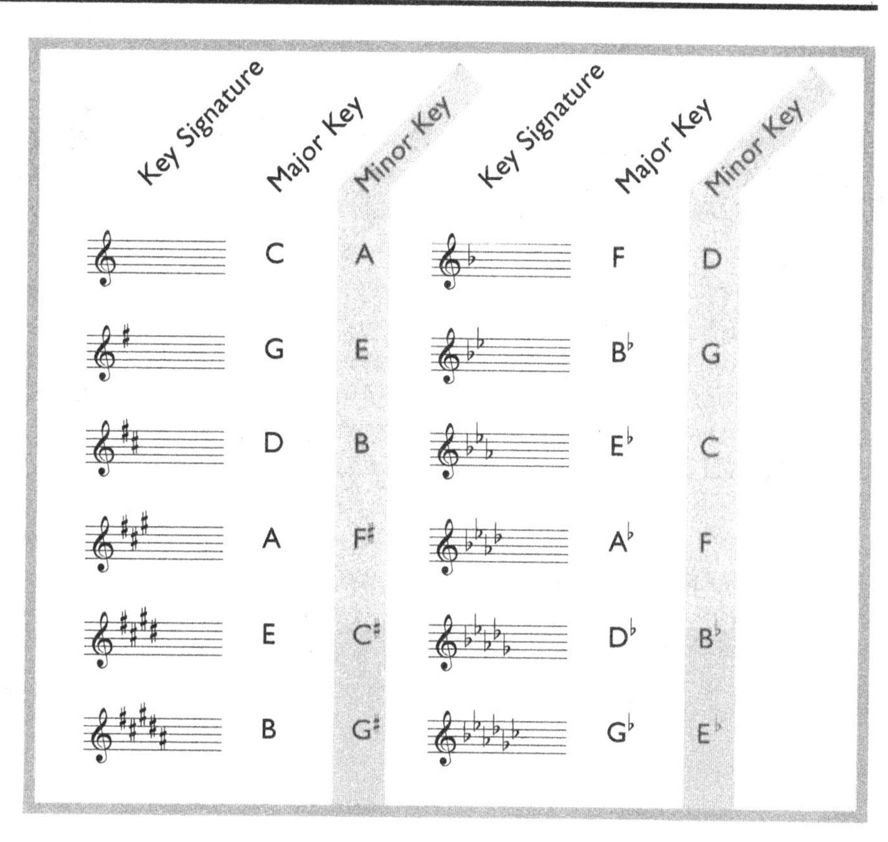

Each key signature is shared by one major and one minor key. We call this relationship *relative*. In other words, we would say that D Minor is the relative minor key to F Major because they share the same key signature: one flat. If the key signature has three sharps, you know the song is in either the key of A Major or F♯ Minor because both the A Major and the F♯ Minor scales contain three sharps. If the song ends on an A Major chord, it is in the key of A Major. If it ends on an F♯min chord, it is in the key of F♯ Minor.

Determining Chord Function

It is important to realize that the same chord can behave very differently in different keys and settings.

In every major and minor key there are seven diatonic chords. We can find out what these chords are by stacking 3rds on top of each note in the scale. Three note stacks will give us triads, four note stacks will give us 7th chords and so on. Notice that if you harmonize each major scale this way, the harmonic pattern stays constant in every key.

Each chord is given a coresponding Roman numeral. Major and Dominant chords will always use upper case numerals (for instance, in a major key: I and IV for major, V7 for Dominant). Minor and diminshed chords will always use lower case (again, in a major key: ii, iii, and vi for minor, vii for min7♭5).

In the harmonized major scale, the first and the fourth chords (I and IV) are always Maj7 chords. The second, third, and sixth chords (ii, iii, vi) are always min7 chords. The fifth chord (V7) is always Dominant and the seventh chord (vii) is always min7♭5 (half diminished). Check out these examples:

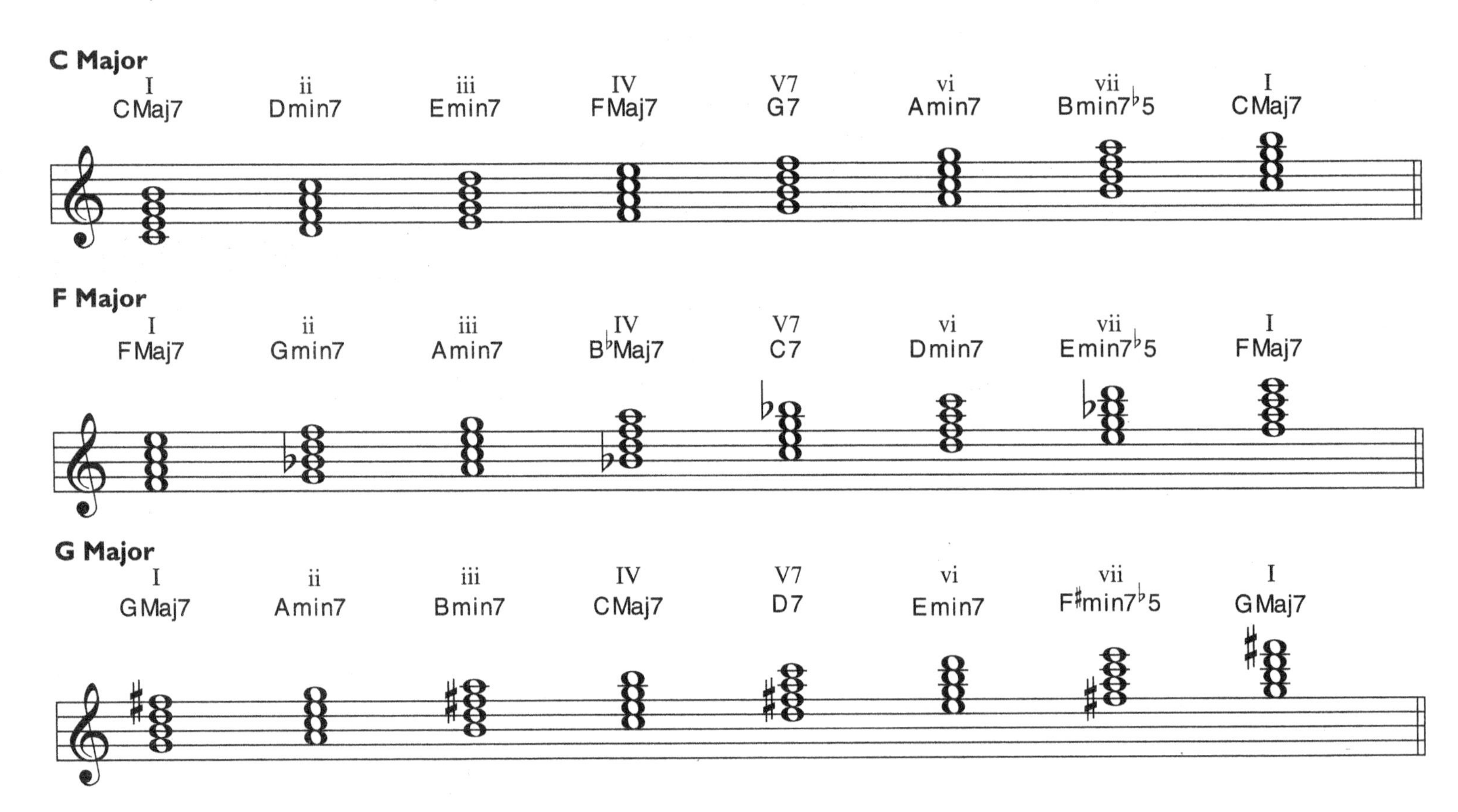

A chord's Roman numeral reveals its function in a key. An FMaj7 played in the key of C (IV) serves a very different role than the same chord in the key of F (I). An Amin7 is the vi chord in the key of C, the iii chord in the key of F and the ii chord in the key of G. What this means is that when learning to improvise over a chord progression, you need to be aware of each chord's function.

Roman numerals can be applied to minor chord progressions as well. Minor chord progressions are based on the chords generated from the melodic and the harmonic minor scales, once again by stacking thirds. In the examples below, these scales are harmonized and the functions of the resulting chords are illustrated.

THE HARMONIZED A MELODIC MINOR SCALE

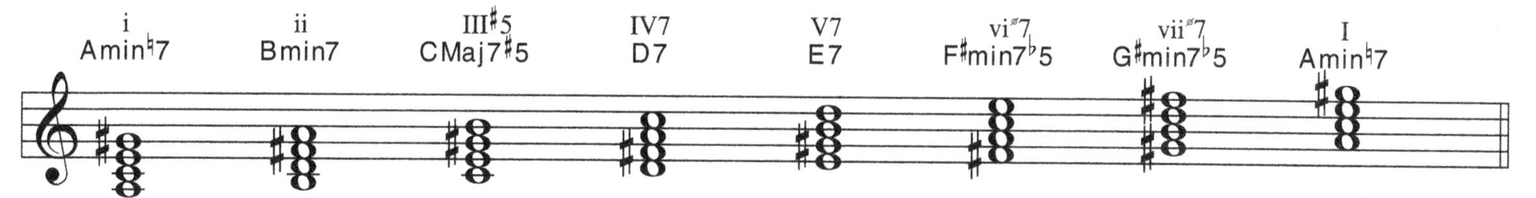

THE HARMONIZED A HARMONIC MINOR SCALE

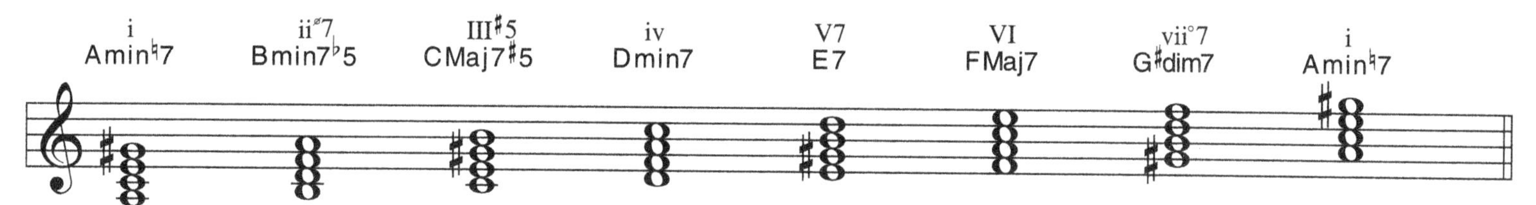

Temporary Key Changes

You should be aware that while some songs stay in one key, some do not. If you are learning a progression that contains chords that fall outside of the key signature, you need to think of these sections as temporary key changes.

The song below seems to be in the key of C because there are no sharps or flats in the key signature. The chord functions are shown above. As the progression continues, we find Gmin7 and C7 which do not belong to the key of C. While FMaj7 does appear in the key of C as the IV chord, it can also be seen as the I chord in the key of F when viewed in the context of the Gmin7 and the C7.

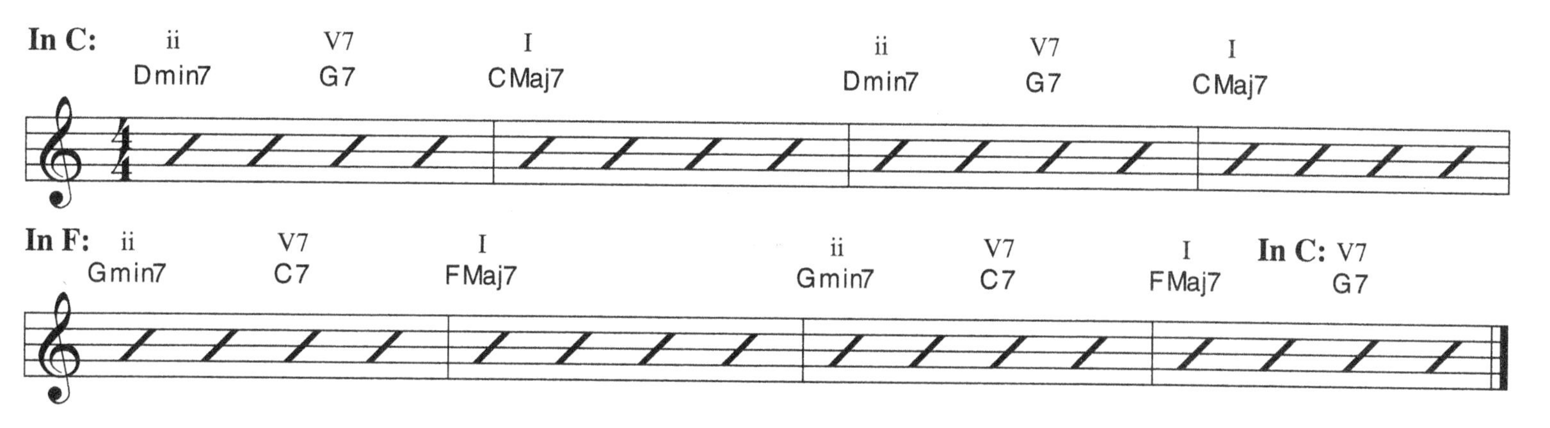

So, from the improvisors point of view, the chord progression has actually changed from the key of C to the key of F (modulated). The Gmin7 functions as a ii chord, the C7 functions as a V7 and the FMaj7 is now a I chord. When the G7 appears at the end, we would view this as the V7 chord in the original key of C.

A working knowledge of diatonic harmony makes it quite simple to determine chord function. In time, you will be able to analyze a chord progression in this way very rapidly.

MAJOR CHORDS
Unaltered

Major, 6, Maj7, Maj9 and Maj13 Chords

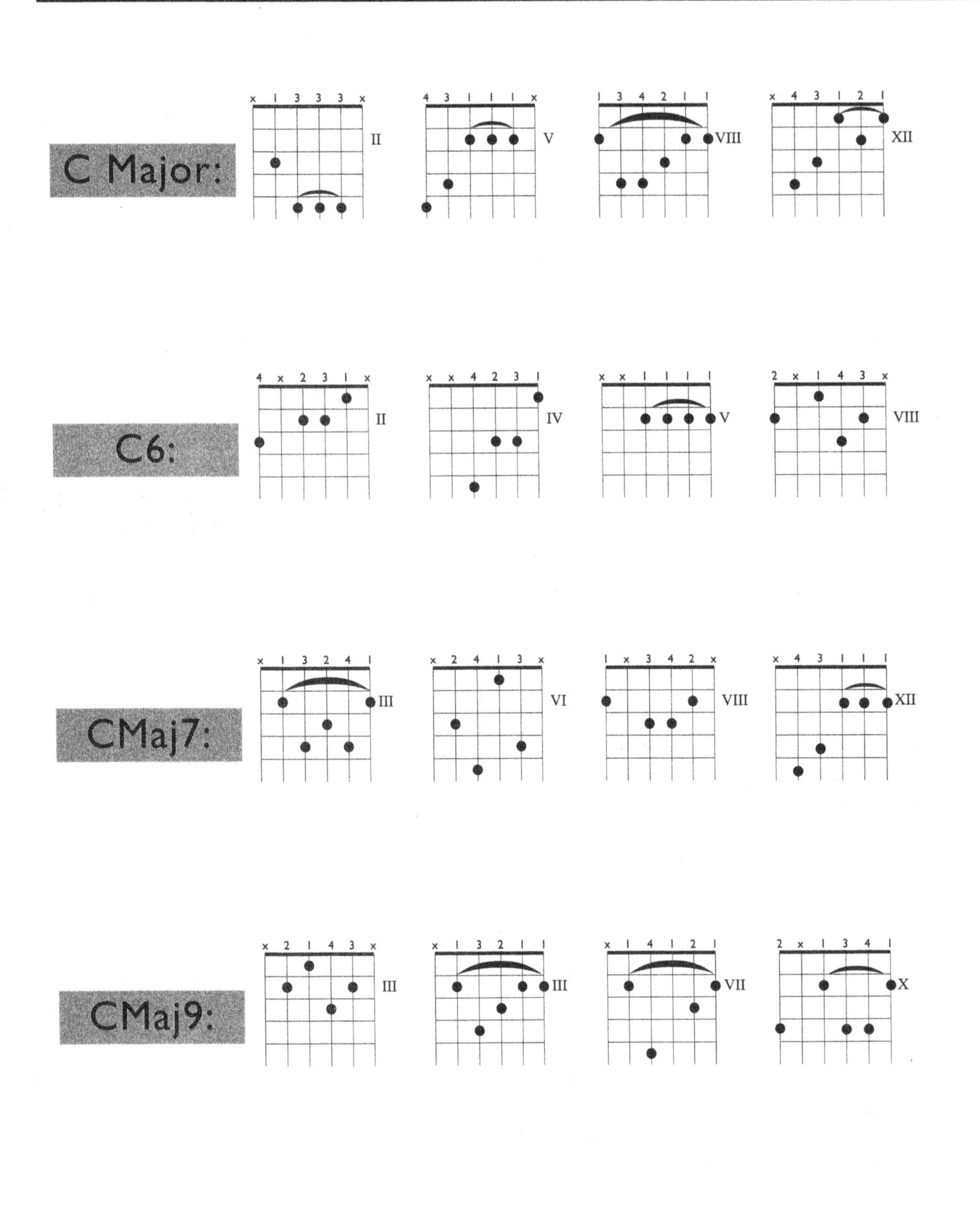

Chord and Scale Chart

Chords	Function	Major or Minor key	Scale or Mode	Starting on...
All unaltered major chords Major, 6, Maj7, Maj9, Maj13	I	Major	Major	The root of the chord
	I or IV	Major	Major Pentatonic	The root of the chord
	I or IV	Major	Major Pentatonic	The 5th of the chord
	IV	Major	Major Pentatonic	The 9th of the chord
	IV	Major	Lydian	The root of the chord
Maj7	VI	Minor	Lydian♯2	The root of the chord

MAJOR

Use a major scale from the root of a I chord in major keys.

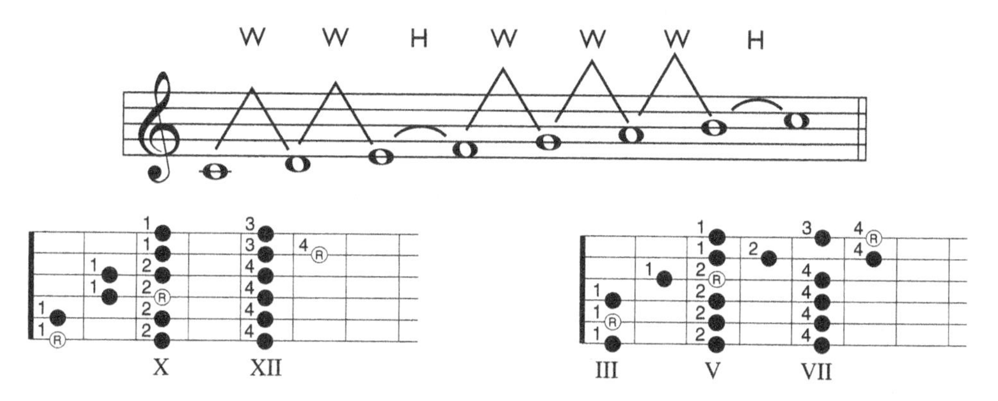

MAJOR PENTATONIC

Use a major pentatonic scale from the root of a I chord or the root of a IV chord in major keys.

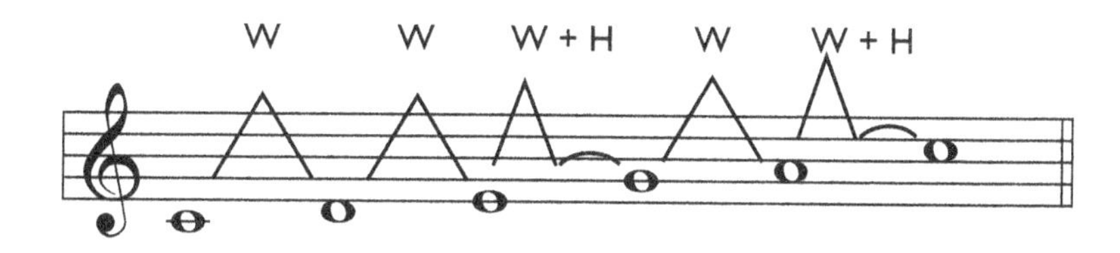

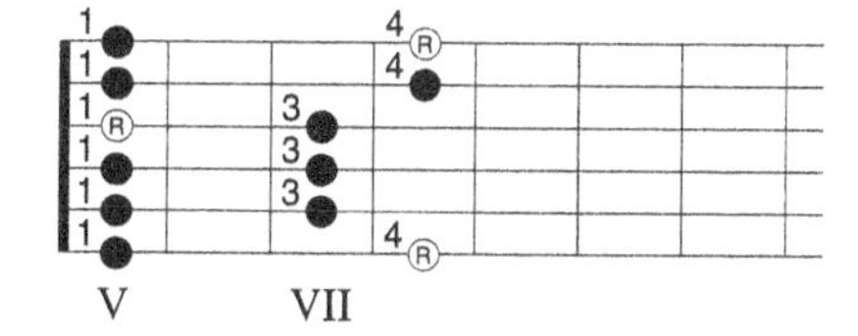

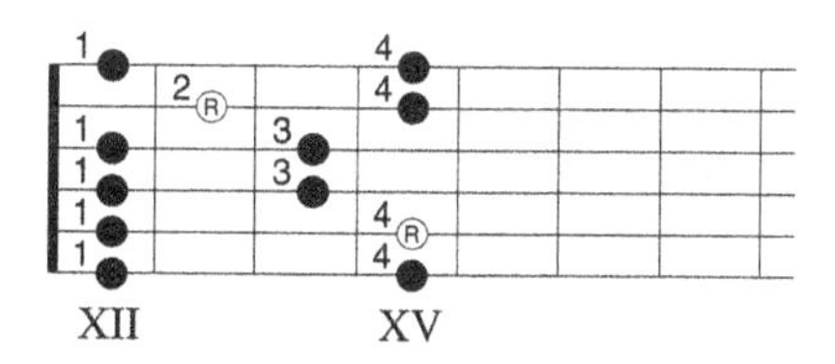

You can also use the major pentatonic scale starting on the 5th of a I or a IV chord in major keys.

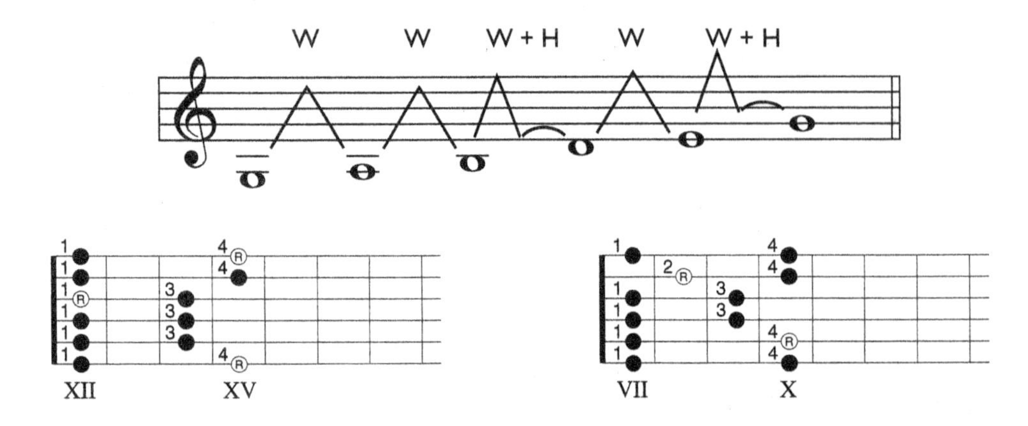

You can also use the major pentatonic scale from the 9th of a IV chord in major keys.

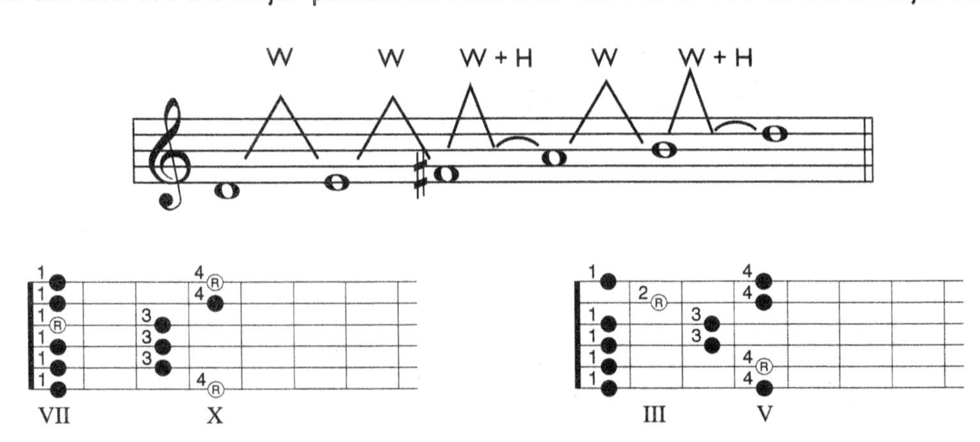

LYDIAN

Use the Lydian mode starting on the root of the IV chord in major keys.

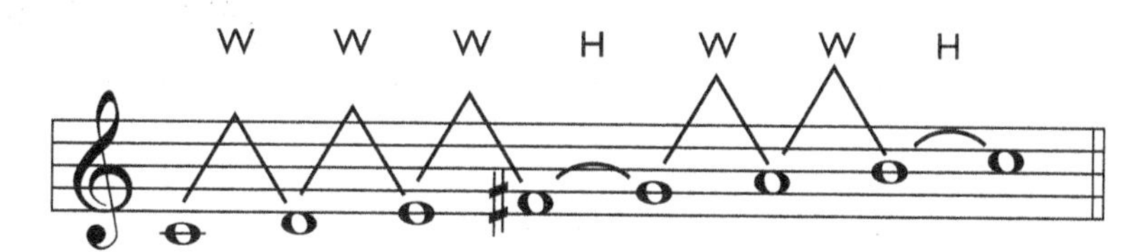

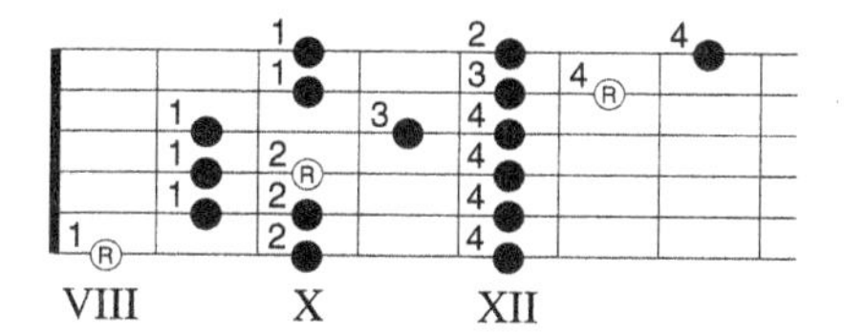

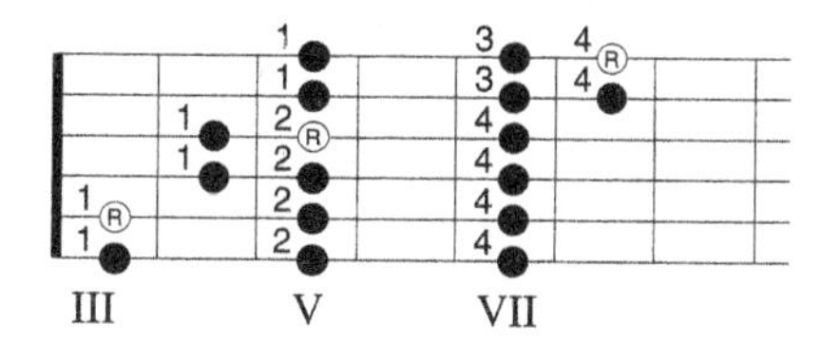

LYDIAN ♯2

Use a Lydian ♯2 mode starting on the root of a Maj7 when it functions as a VI chord in a minor key.

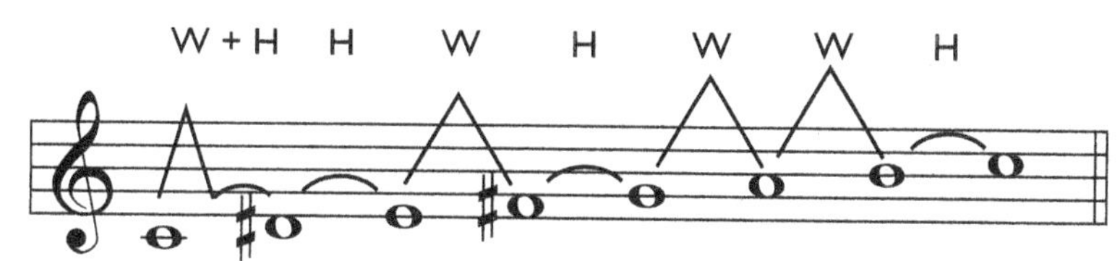

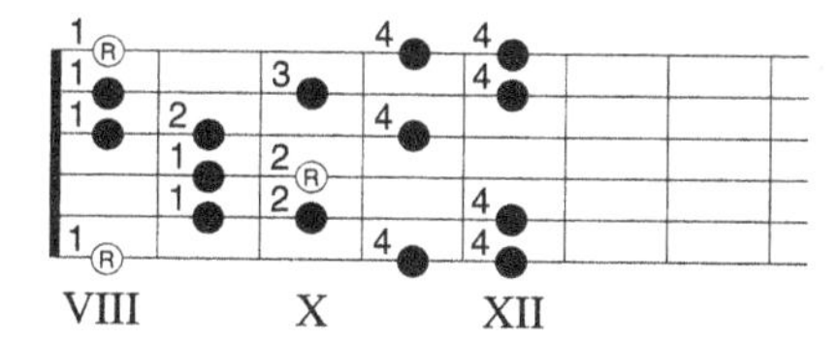

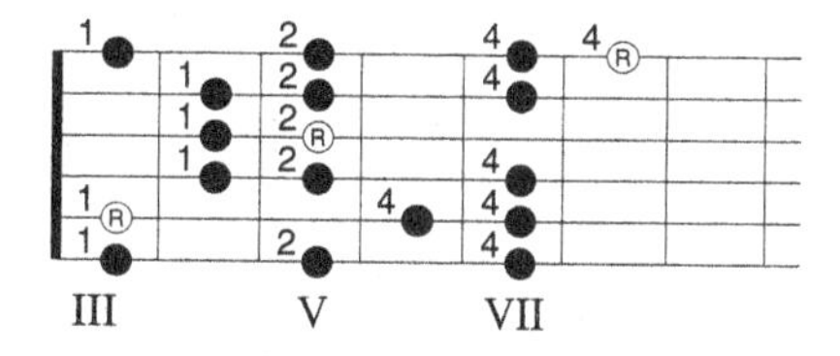

MAJOR CHORDS
Altered

Maj7#5 Chords

CMaj7#5:

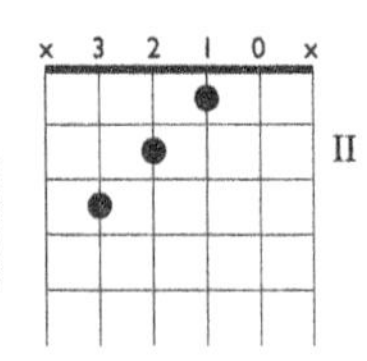

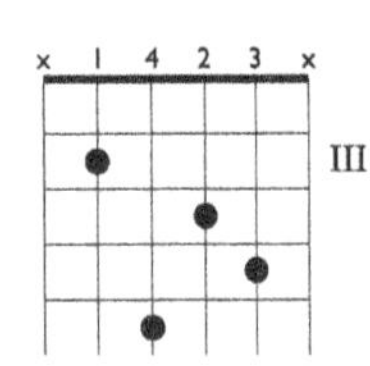

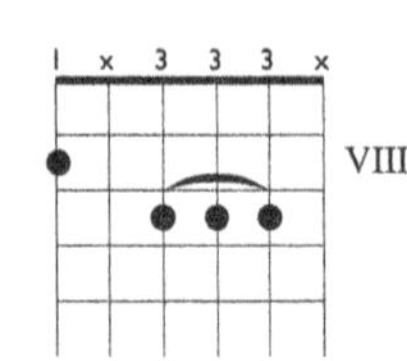

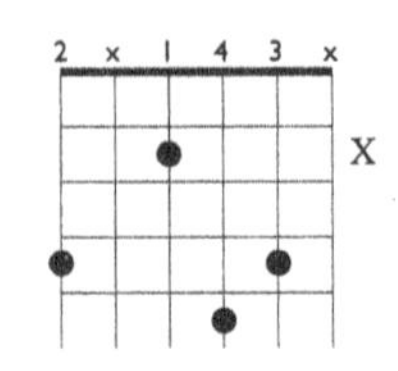

Chord and Scale Chart

Chords	Function	Major or Minor key	Scale or Mode	Starting on...
Maj7#5	Any	Both	Lydian Augmented	The root of the chord
	Any	Both	Ionian #5	The root of the chord

LYDIAN AUGMENTED

Use a Lydian Augmented mode starting on the root of a Maj7#5 chord.

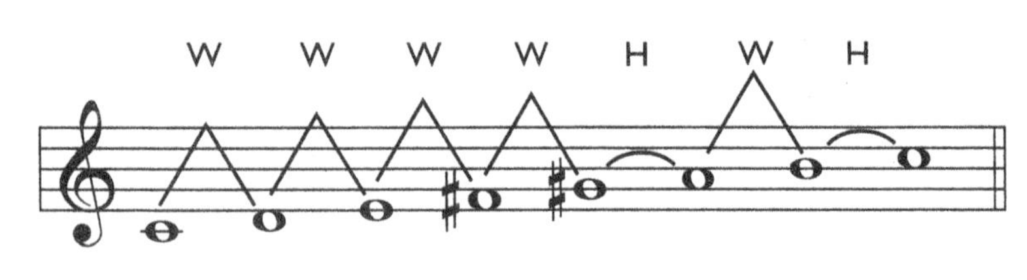

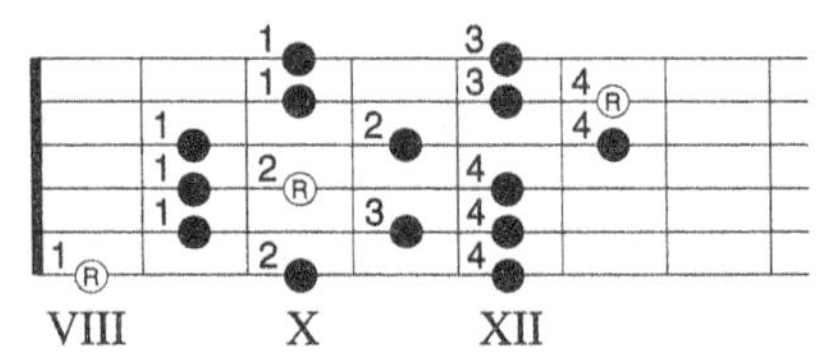

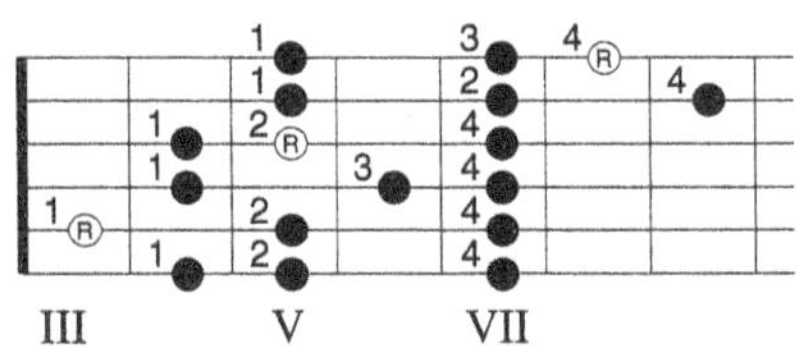

IONIAN #5

Use the Ionian #5 mode starting on the root of a Maj7#5 chord.

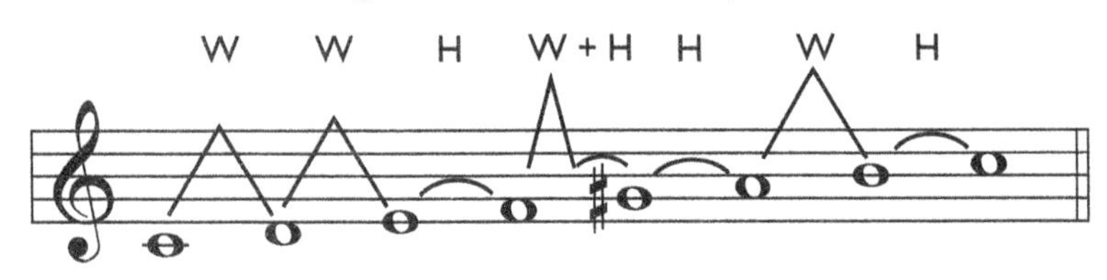

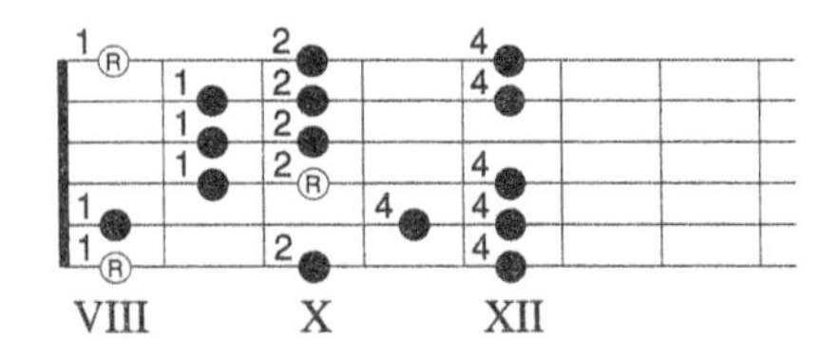

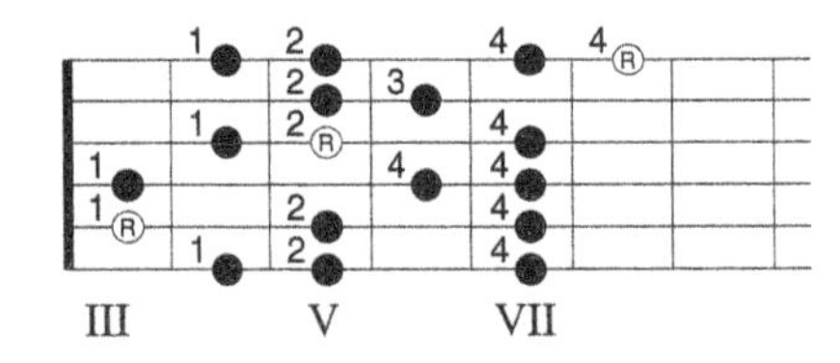

Maj7♭5, Maj7#11 and Maj9#11 Chords

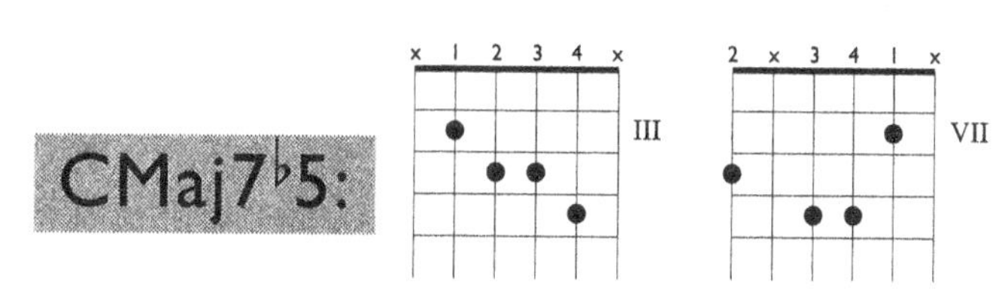

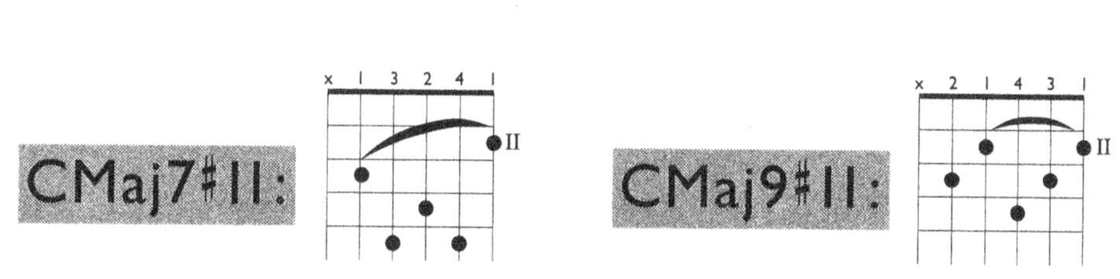

Chord and Scale Chart

Chords	Function	Major or Minor key	Scale or Mode	Starting on...
Maj7♭5, Maj7#11, Maj9#11	Any	Both	Major Pentatonic	The 9th of the chord
	Any	Both	Lydian	The root of the chord

MAJOR PENTATONIC *(from the 9th)*

Use a major pentatonic scale starting on the 9th of a Maj7♭5, Maj7#11 or Maj9#11 chord.

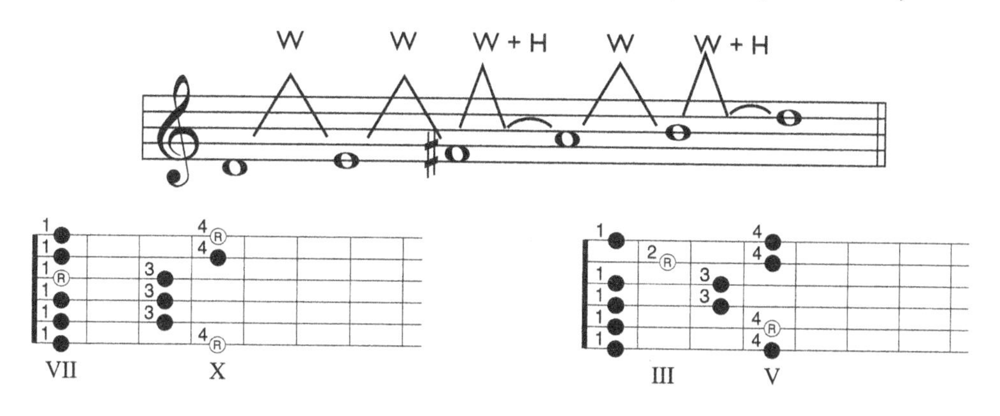

LYDIAN

Use the Lydian mode starting on the root of a Maj7♭5, Maj7#11 or Maj9#11 chord.

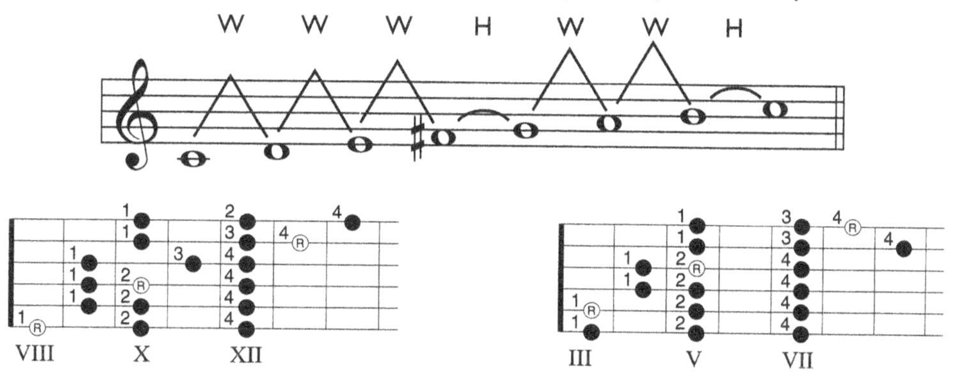

Maj7#5#11 Chords

CMaj7♯5♯11:

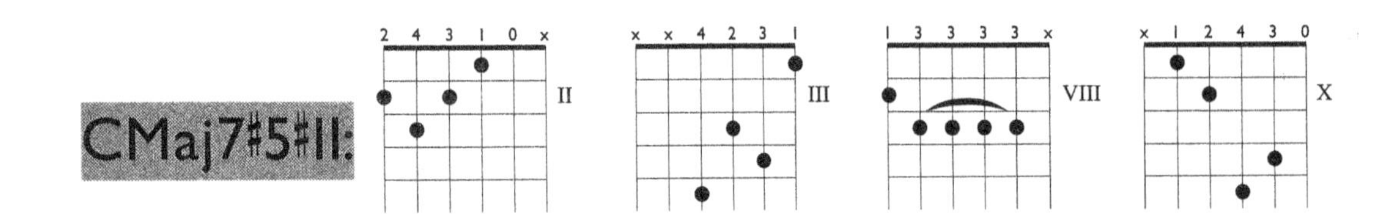

Chord and Scale Chart

Chords	Function	Major or Minor key	Scale or Mode	Starting on...
Maj7♯5♯11	Any	Both	Lydian Augmented	The 9th of the chord

LYDIAN AUGMENTED

Use the Lydian Augmented mode starting on the root of a Maj7♯5♯11 chord.

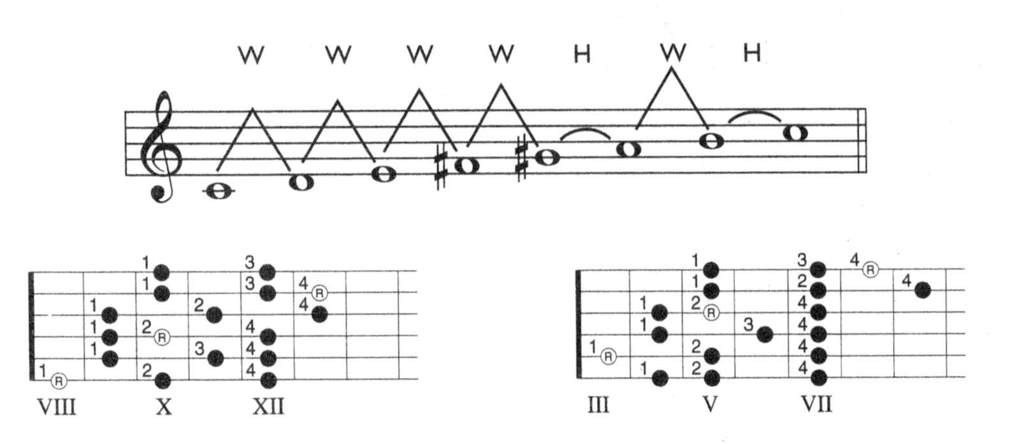

DOMINANT CHORDS

Unaltered

7, 9, 11, 13 and 7sus4 Chords

C7:

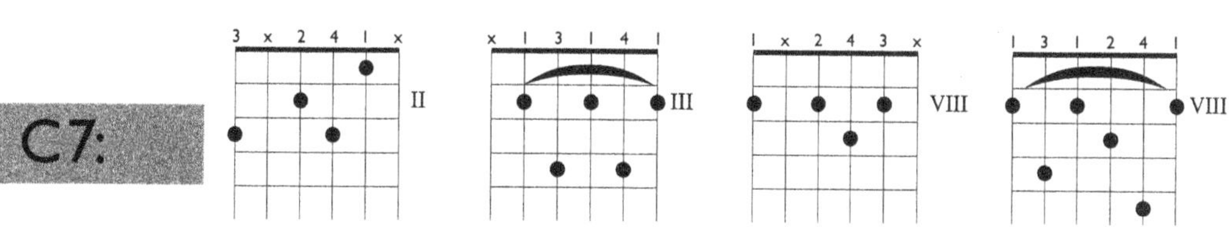

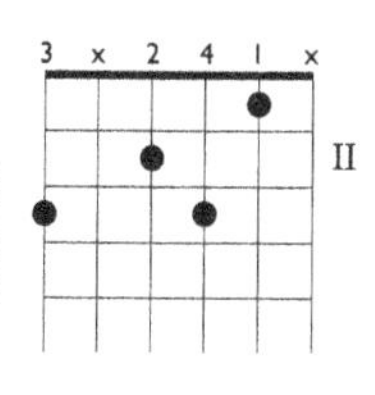
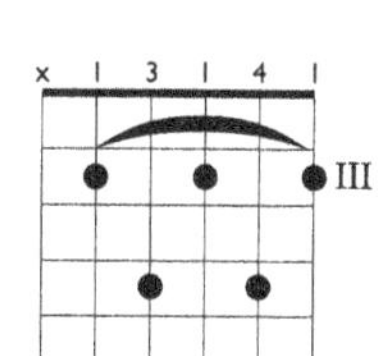
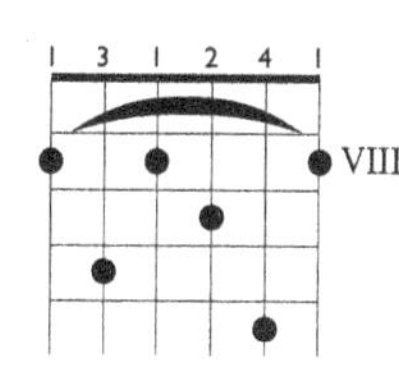

C9:

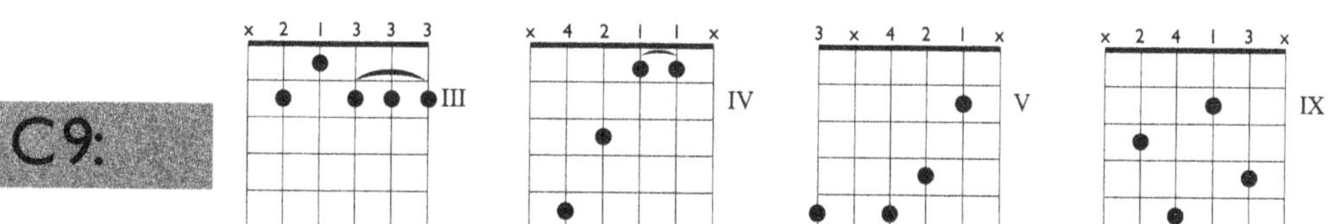

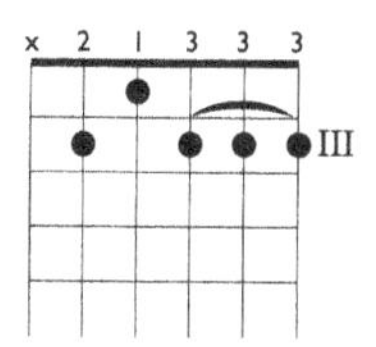
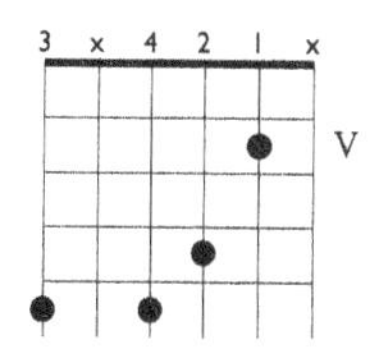
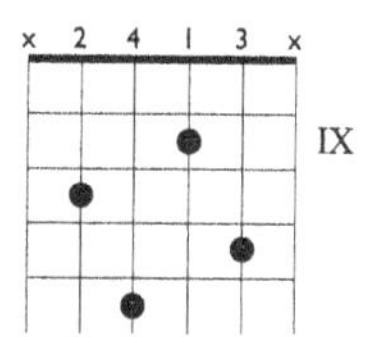

C11:

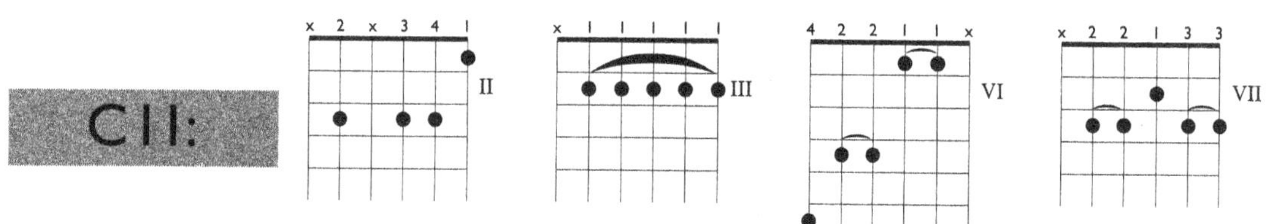

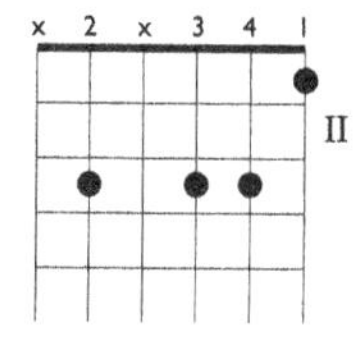
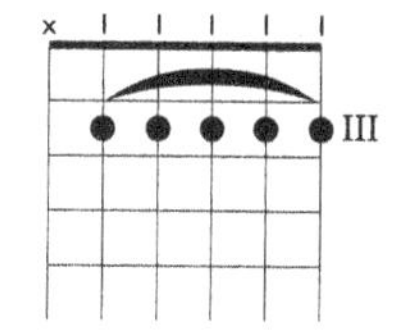
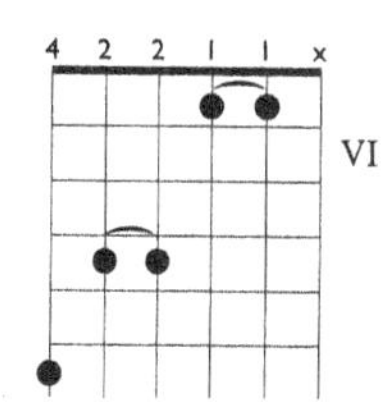

C13:

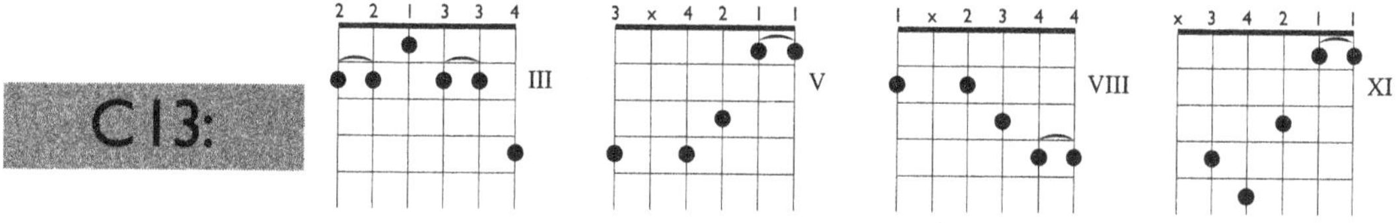

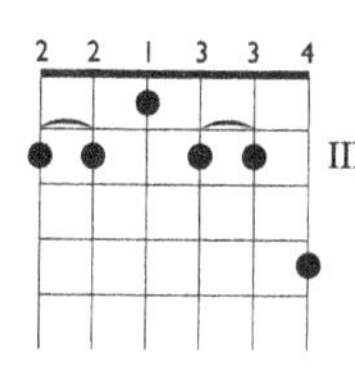
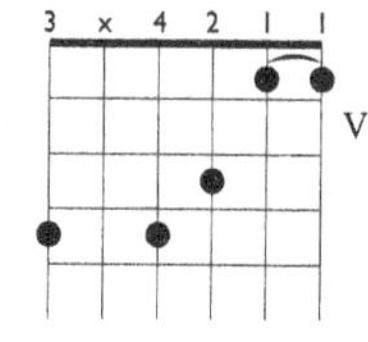
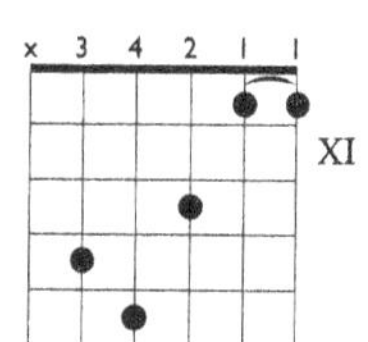

C7sus4:

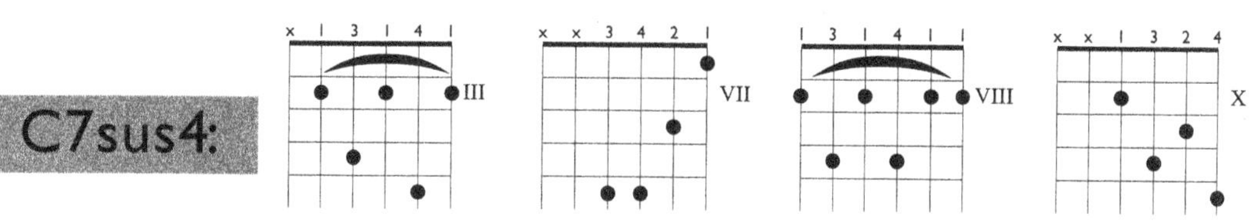

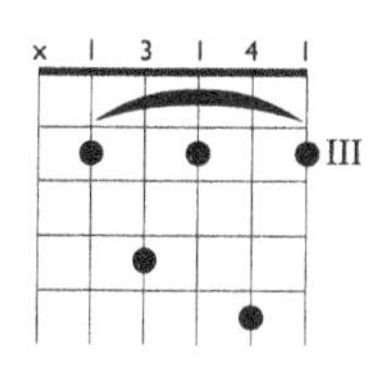
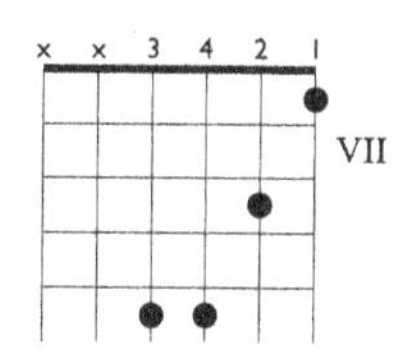
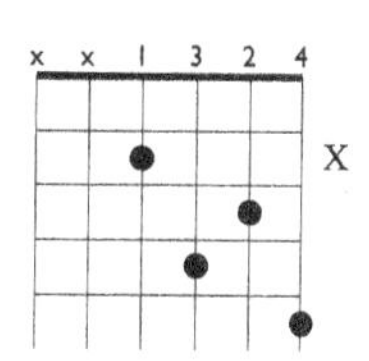

Chord and Scale Chart

Chords	Function	Major or Minor key	Scale or Mode	Starting on...
All unaltered dominant chords: 7, 9, 11, 13, and 7sus4 *except where marked* *	Any	Major	Major Pentatonic	The root of the chord
	Any	Major	Major Pentatonic	The 4th of the chord
	Any	Major	Minor Pentatonic	The root of the chord
	Any	Major	Minor Pentatonic	The 5th of the chord
	Any	Major	Blues	The root of the chord
	Any	Major	Mixolydian	The root of the chord
	IV	Minor	Lydian ♭7* **not good for 11 or 7sus4 chords*	The root of the chord
	V	Minor	Mixolydian ♭6* **not good for 13 chords*	The root of the chord
	V	Minor	Phrygian Dominant* **not good for 9 chords*	The root of the chord
7sus4	Any	Both	Dorian	The root of the chord
7sus4	Any	Both	Dorian	The 5th of the chord

MAJOR PENTATONIC

Use a major pentatonic scale starting on the root of any dominant chord in a major key.

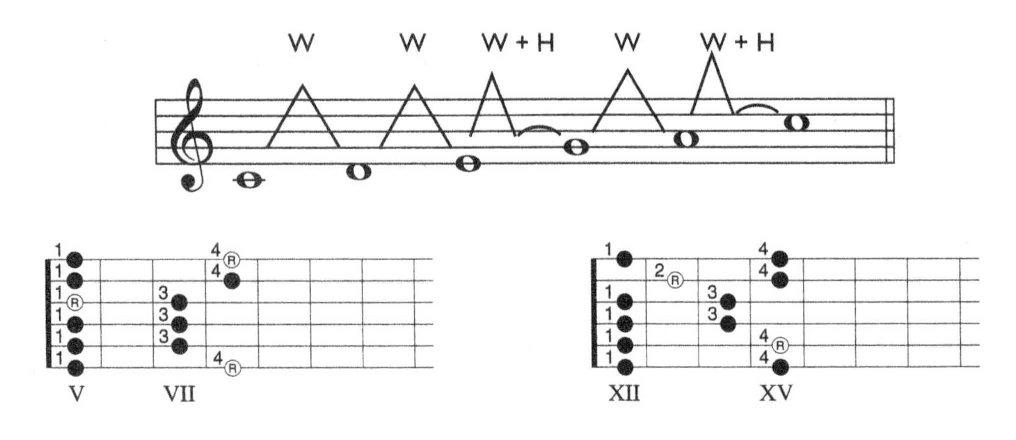

You can also use a major pentatonic scale starting on the 4th of any dominant chord in a major key.

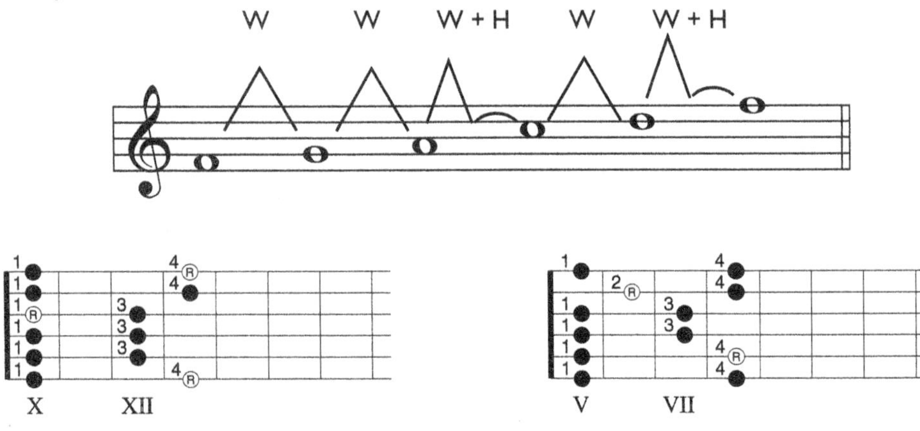

MINOR PENTATONIC

Use a minor pentatonic scale starting on the root of any dominant chord in a major key.

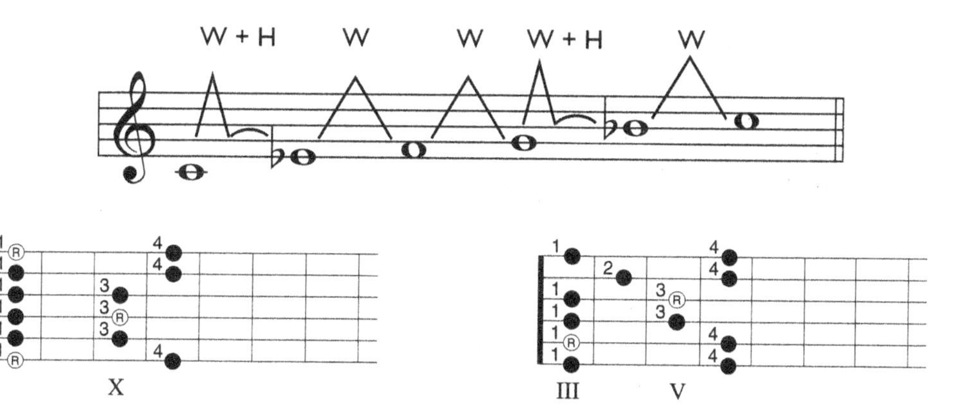

You can also use a minor pentatonic scale starting on the 5th of any dominant chord in a major key.

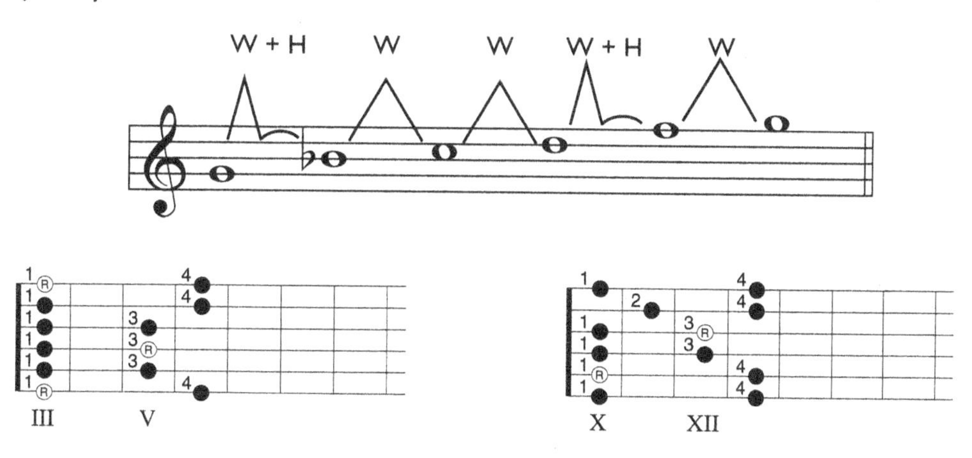

BLUES SCALE

Use a blues scale starting on the root of any dominant chord in a major key.

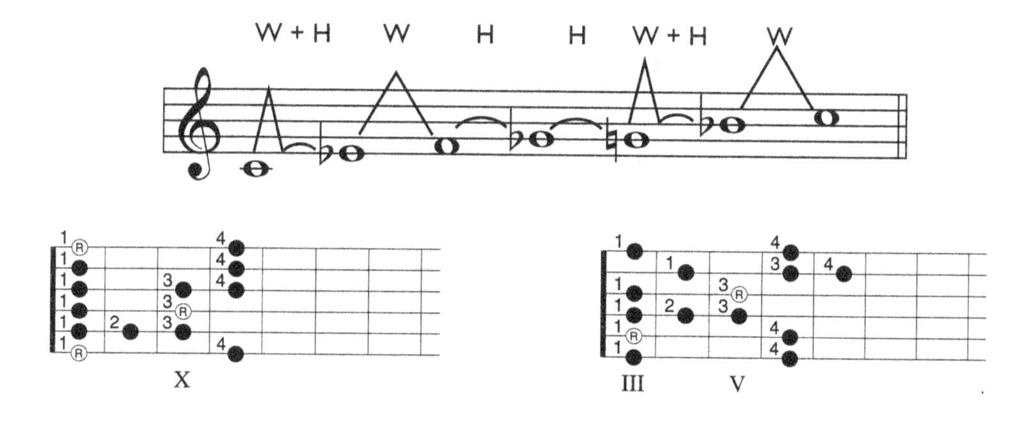

MIXOLYDIAN

Use the Mixolydian mode starting on the root of the chord.

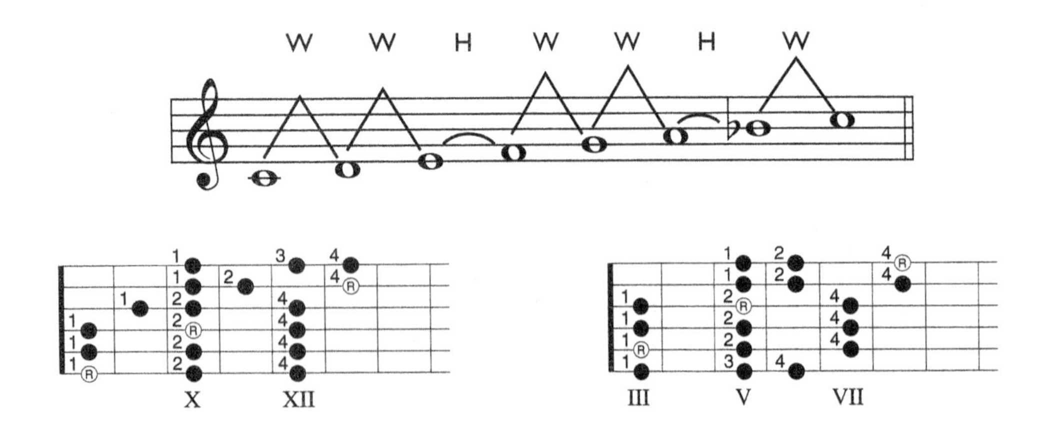

LYDIAN ♭7

Use the Lydian ♭7 mode starting on the root any dominant chord other than an 11 chord.

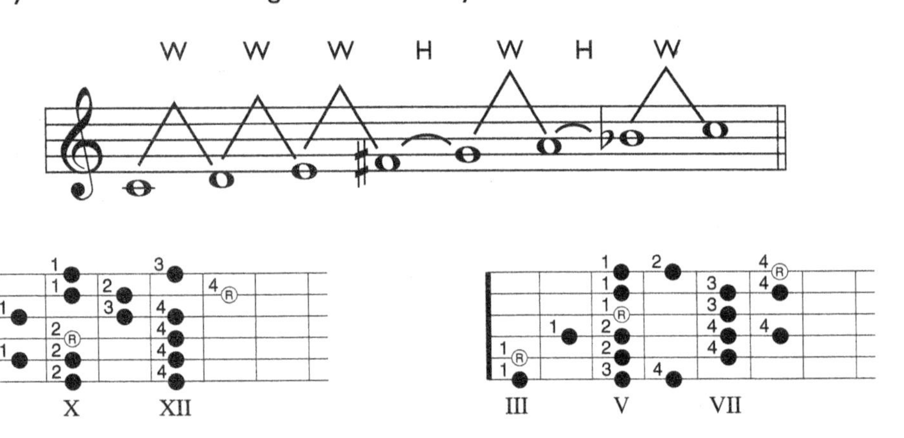

MIXOLYDIAN ♭6

Use the Mixolydian ♭6 mode starting on the root any dominant chord other than a 13 chord.

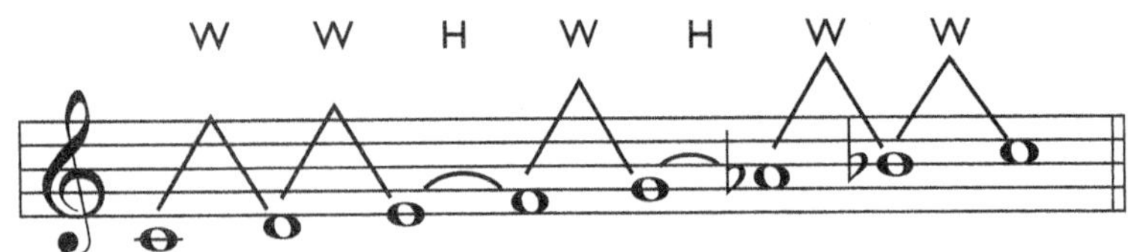

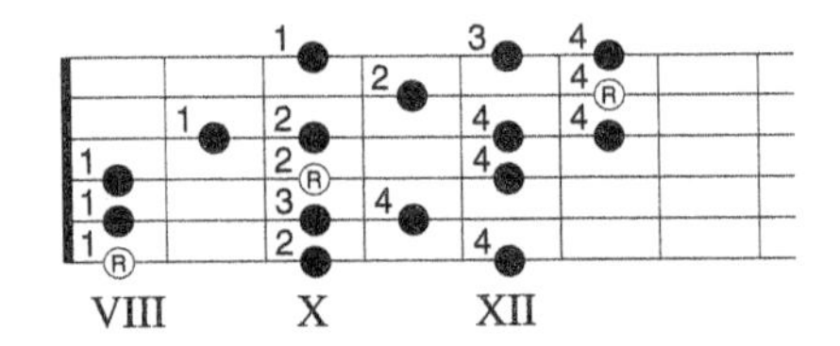

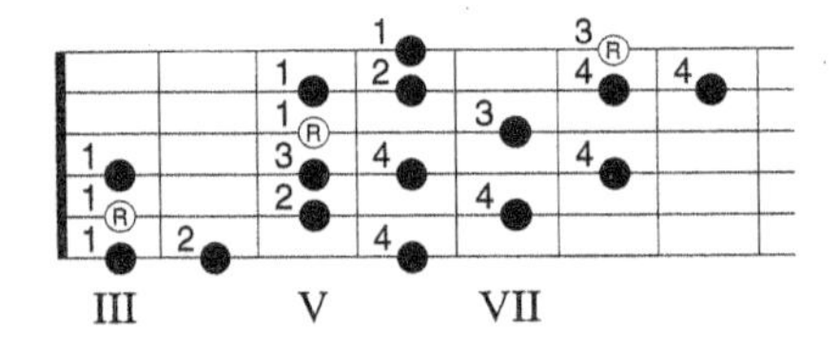

PHRYGIAN DOMINANT

Use the Phrygian dominant mode starting on the root of any dominant chord, with the exception of 9 chords.

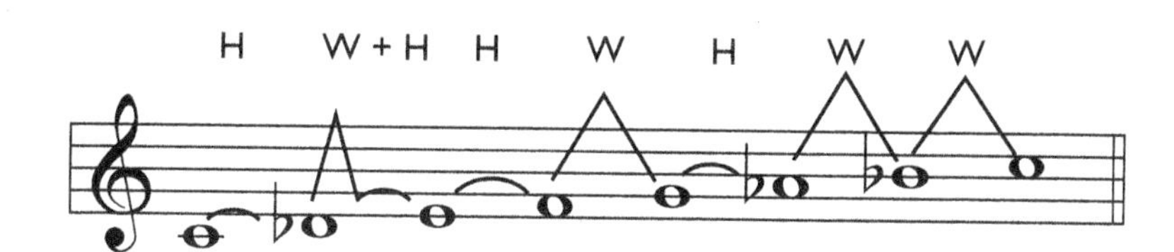

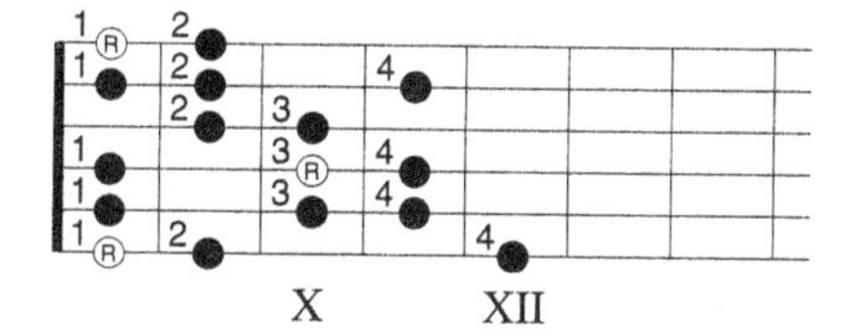

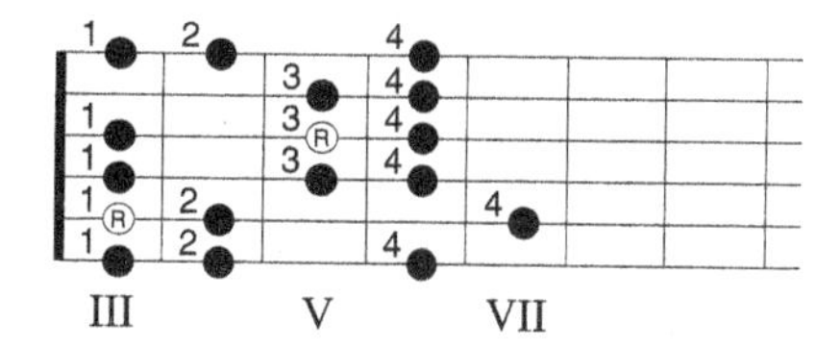

DORIAN

Use the Dorian mode starting on the root of a 7sus4 chord.

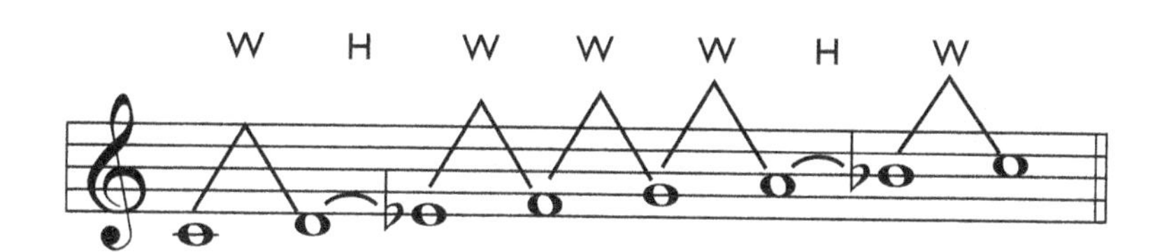

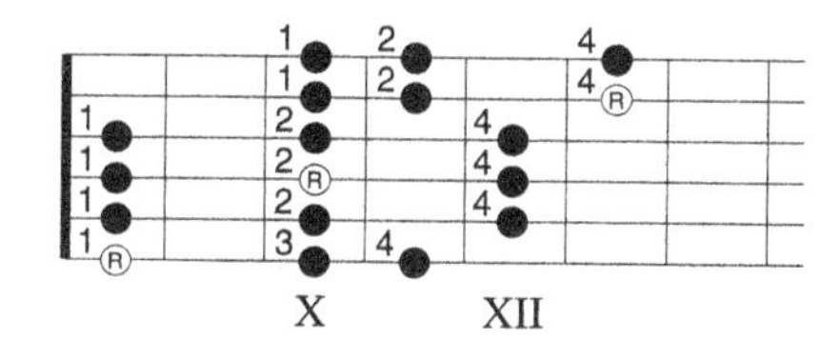

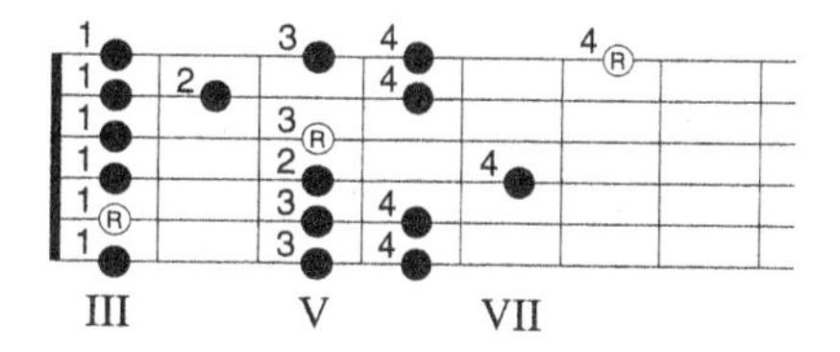

You can also use the Dorian mode starting from the 5th of a 7sus4 chord.

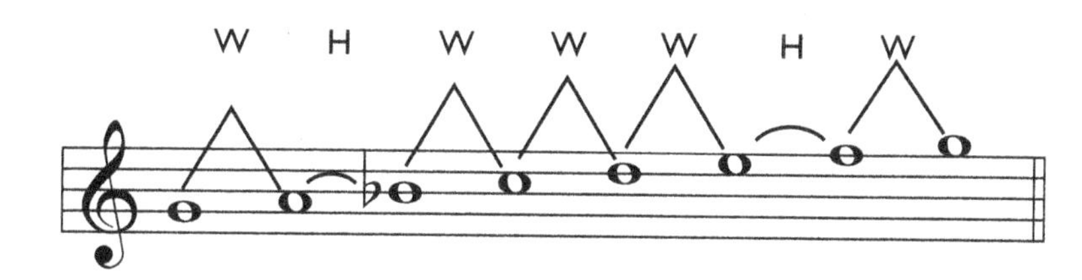

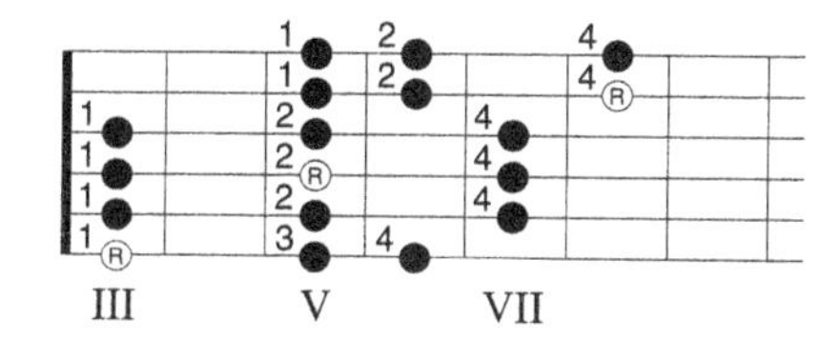

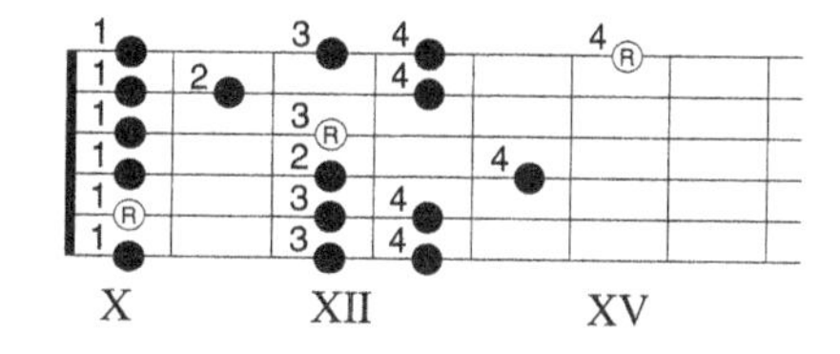

DOMINANT CHORDS

Altered

7♭5 Chords

C7♭5:

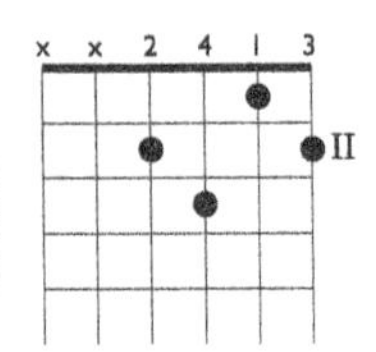

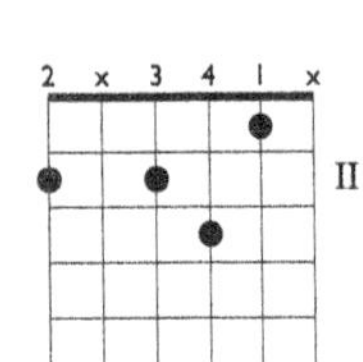

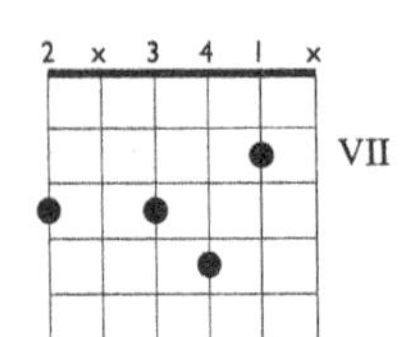

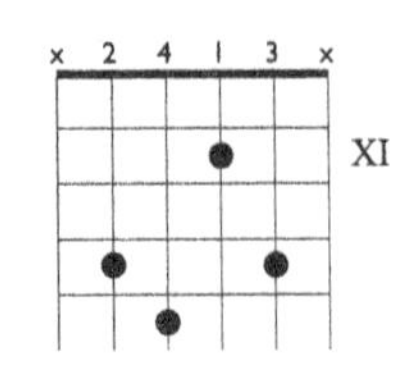

Chord and Scale Chart

Chords	Function	Major or Minor key	Scale or Mode	Starting on...
7♭5	Any	Both	Whole Tone	The root of the chord
	Any	Both	Whole Tone	The 3rd of the chord
	Any	Both	Whole Tone	The ♭5 of the chord
	Any	Both	Whole Tone	The ♭7 of the chord
	Any	Both	Diminished	½ step above the root of the chord
	Any	Both	Lydian ♭7	The root of the chord
	Any	Both	Super Locrian	The root of the chord
	Any	Both	Blues	The root of the chord

WHOLE TONE

Use a whole tone scale from the root of a 7♭5 chord.

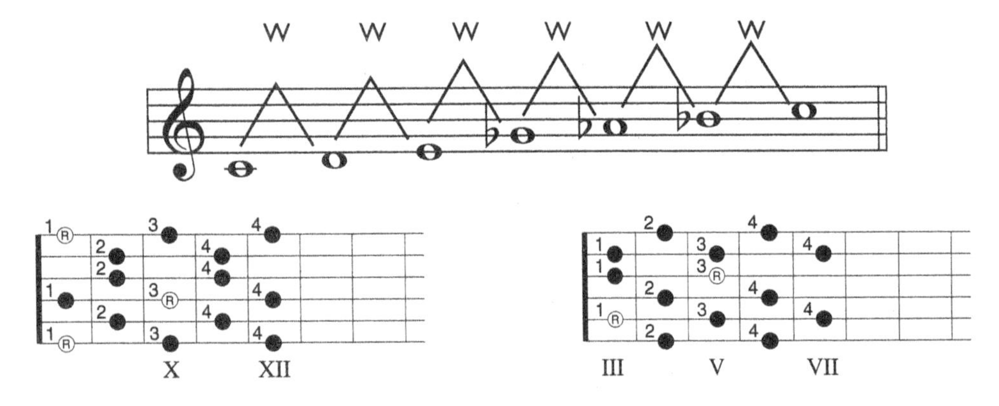

Use a whole tone scale from the 3rd of a 7♭5 chord.

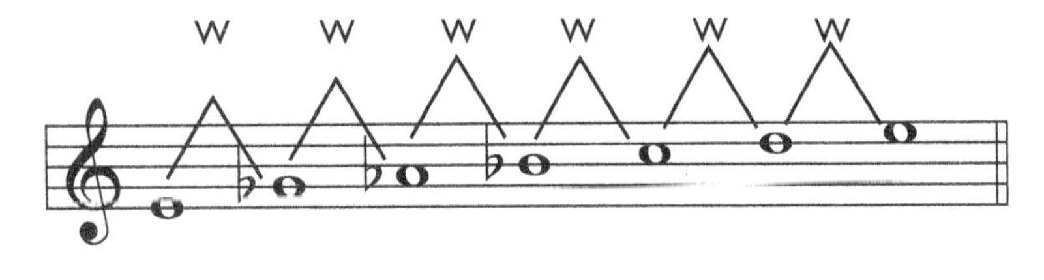

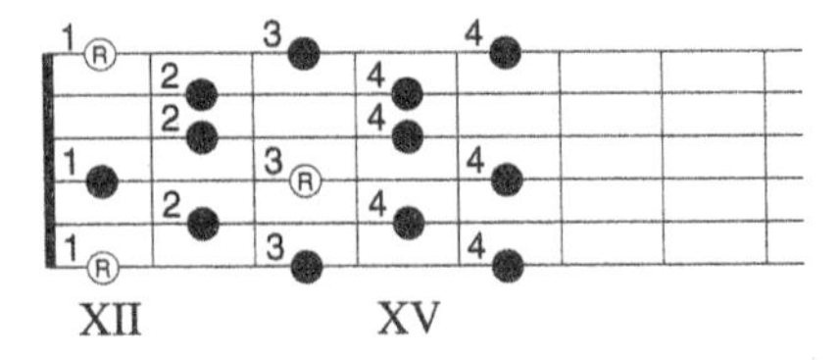

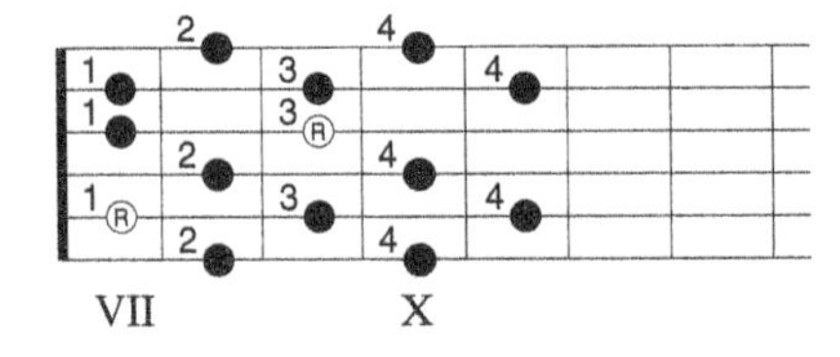

LYDIAN ♭7

Use a Lydian ♭7 scale starting on the root of a 7♭5 chord.

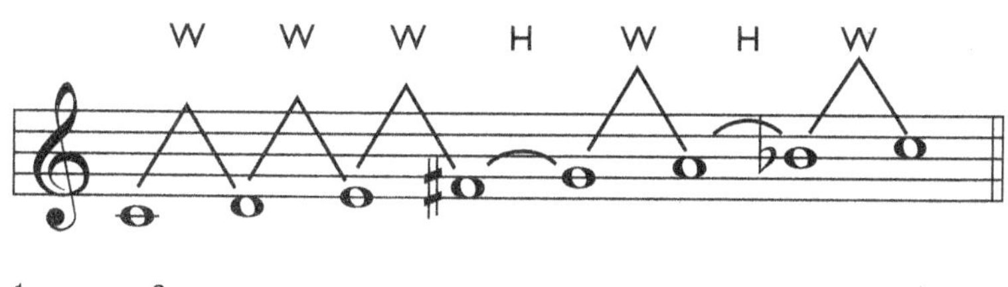

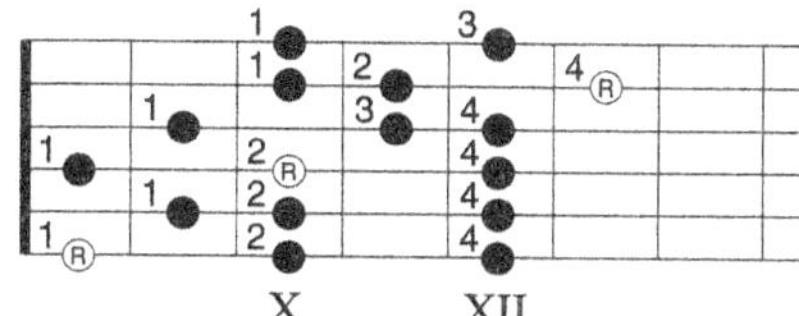

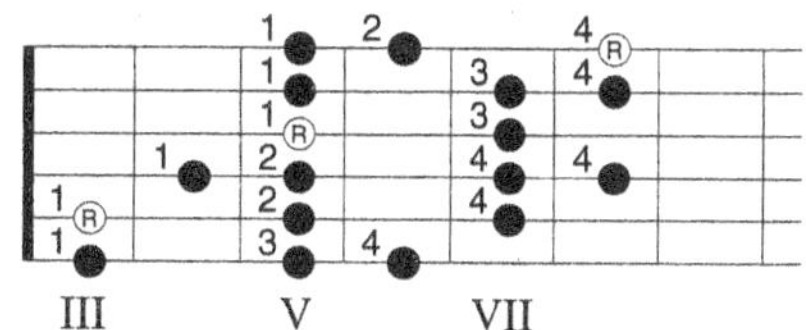

SUPER LOCRIAN

Use the super Locrian mode starting on the root of a 7♭5 chord.

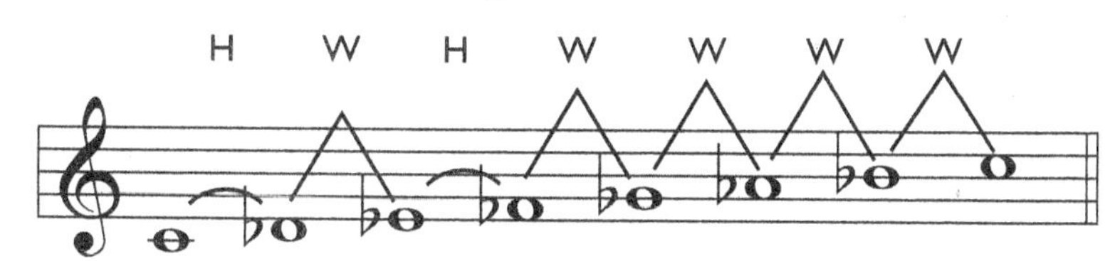

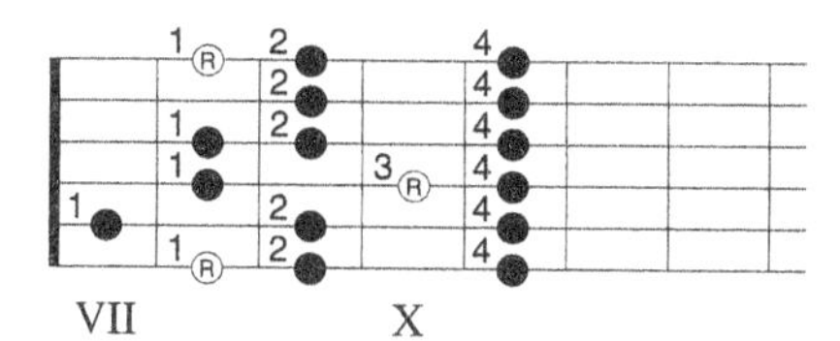

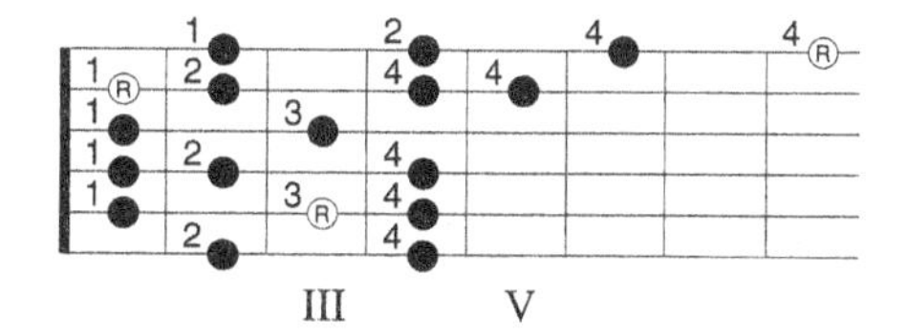

BLUES

Use a blues scale starting on the root of a 7♭5 chord.

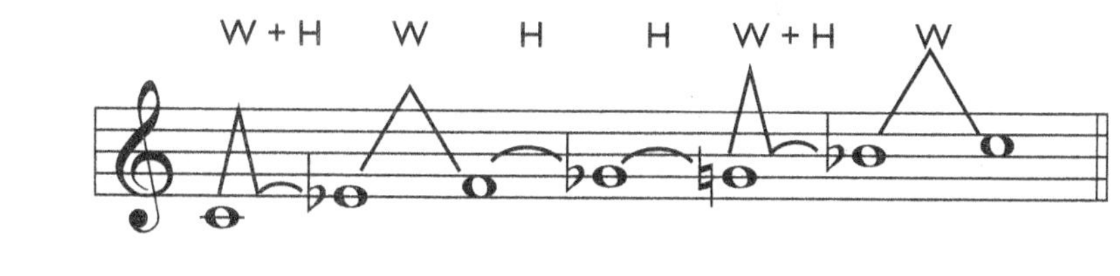

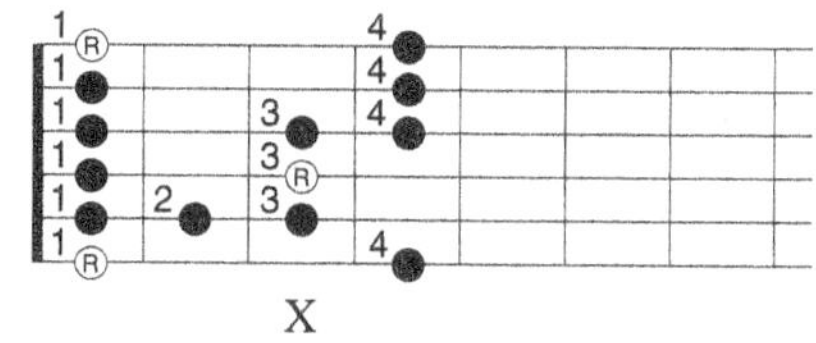

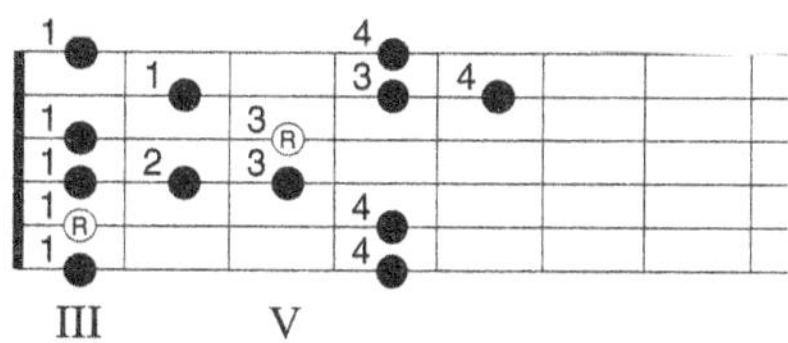

LYDIAN ♭7

Use a Lydian ♭7 scale starting on the root of a 7♭5 chord.

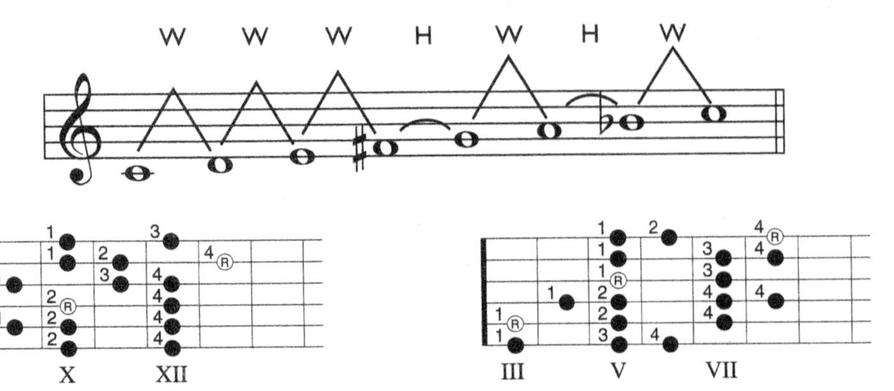

SUPER LOCRIAN

Use the super Locrian mode starting on the root of a 7♭5 chord.

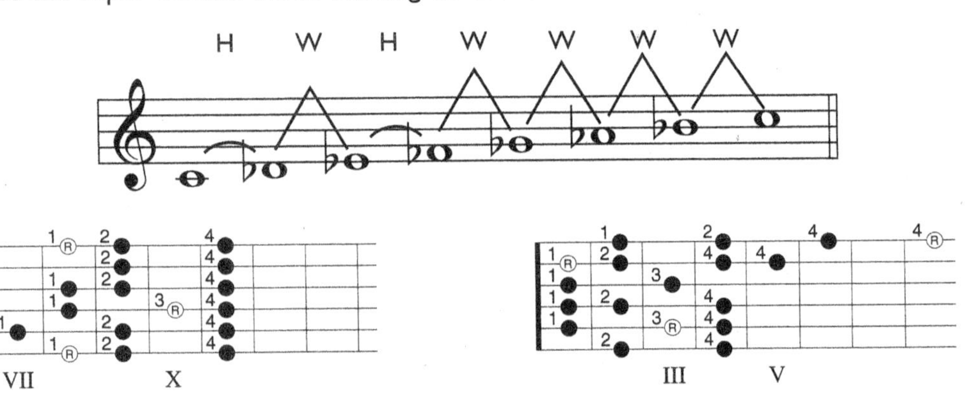

BLUES

Use a blues scale starting on the root of a 7♭5 chord.

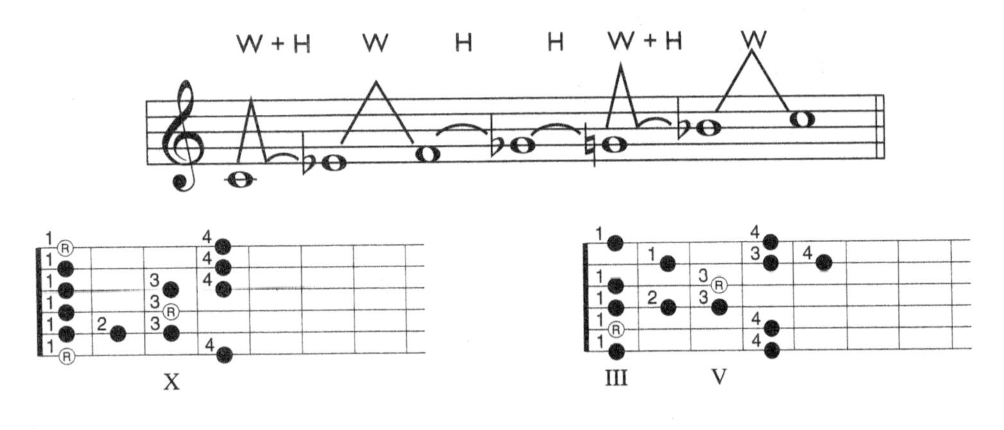

7♯5 and 9♯5 Chords

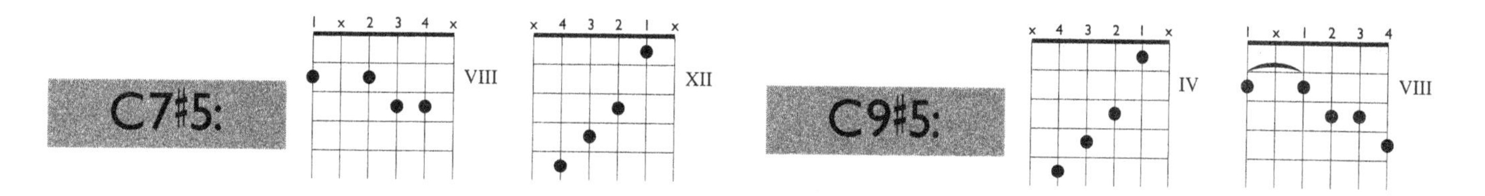

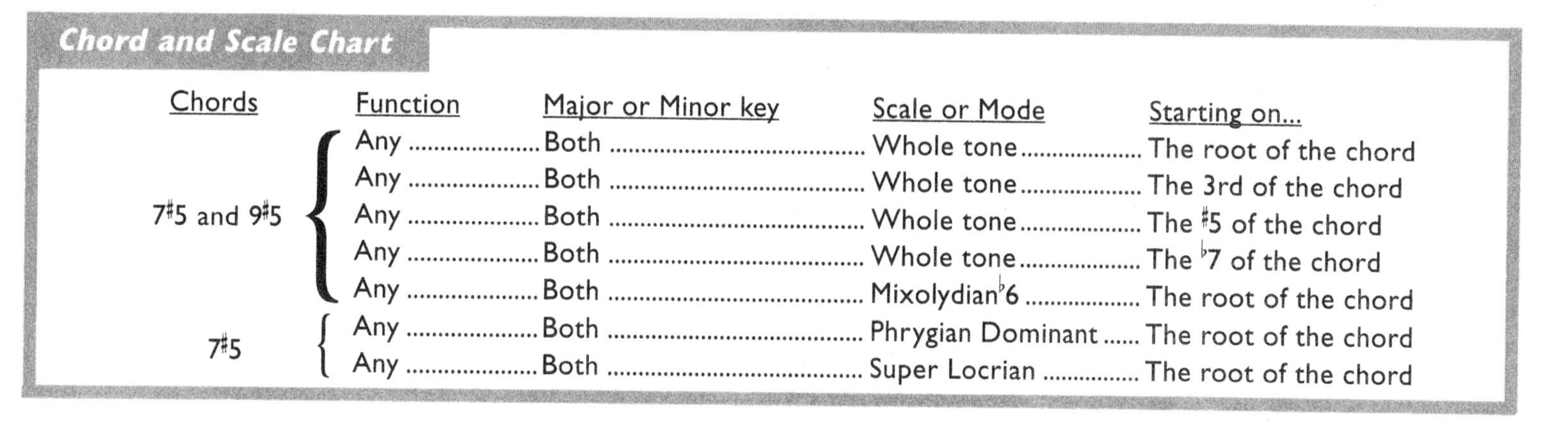

Chord and Scale Chart

Chords	Function	Major or Minor key	Scale or Mode	Starting on...
7♯5 and 9♯5	Any	Both	Whole tone	The root of the chord
	Any	Both	Whole tone	The 3rd of the chord
	Any	Both	Whole tone	The ♯5 of the chord
	Any	Both	Whole tone	The ♭7 of the chord
	Any	Both	Mixolydian♭6	The root of the chord
7♯5	Any	Both	Phrygian Dominant	The root of the chord
	Any	Both	Super Locrian	The root of the chord

WHOLE TONE

Use a whole tone scale starting on the root of a 7♯5 or 9♯5 chord.

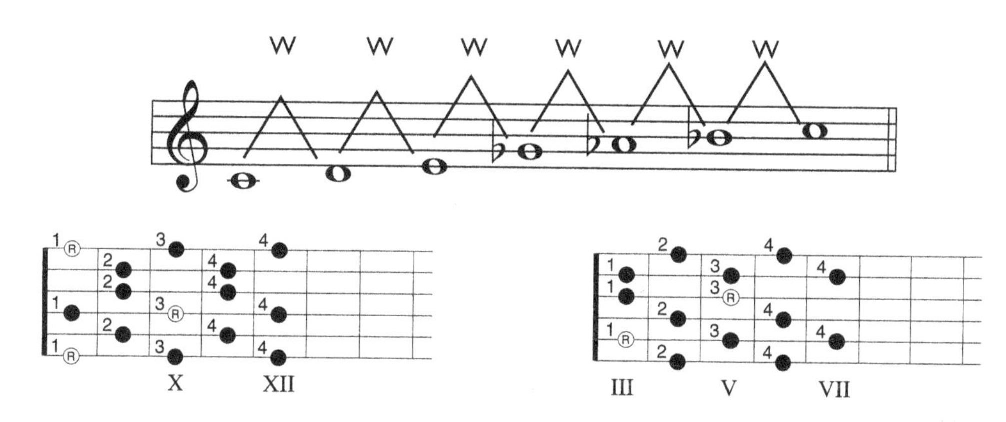

You can also use a whole tone scale starting on the 3rd of a 7♯5 or 9♯5 chord.

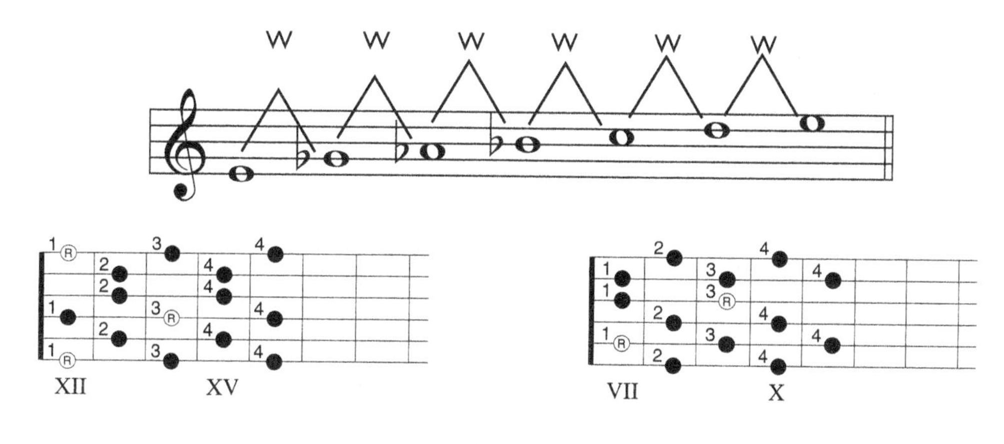

(continued)

Or, use a whole tone scale starting on the ♯5 of a 7♯5 or 9♯5 chord.

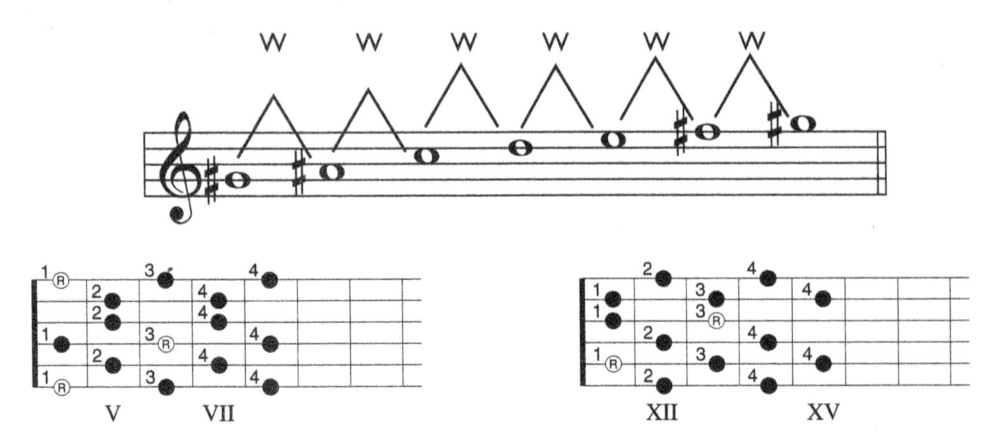

It is also possible to use a whole tone scale starting on the ♭7 of a 7♯5 or 9♯5 chord.

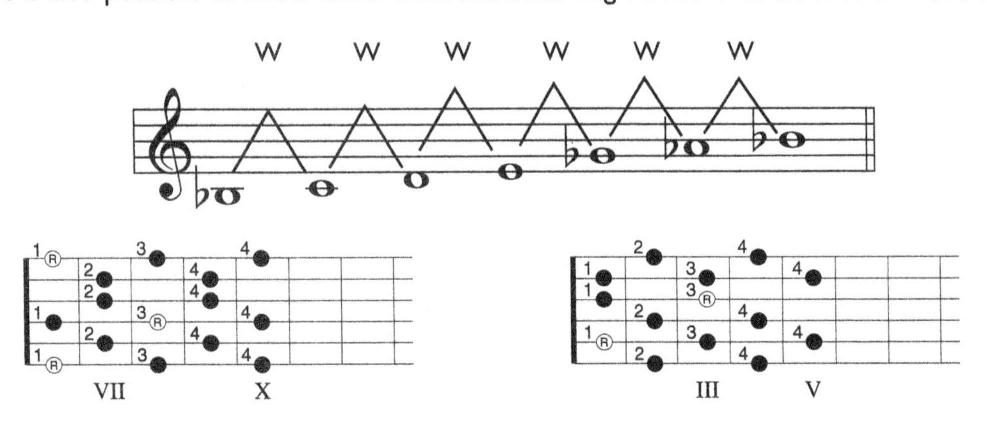

SUPER LOCRIAN

Use the super Locrian mode starting on the root of a 7♯5 chord.

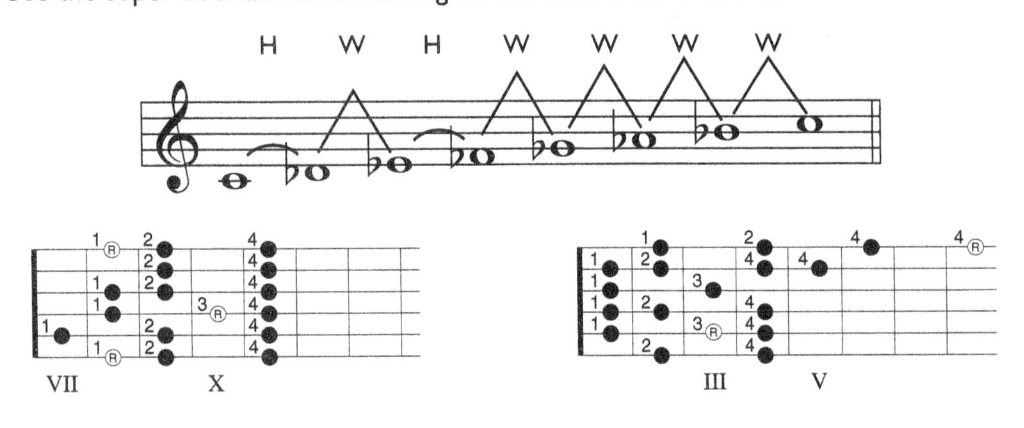

MIXOLYDIAN ♭6

Use the Mixolydian ♭6 mode starting on the root of a 7♯5 or 9♯5 chord.

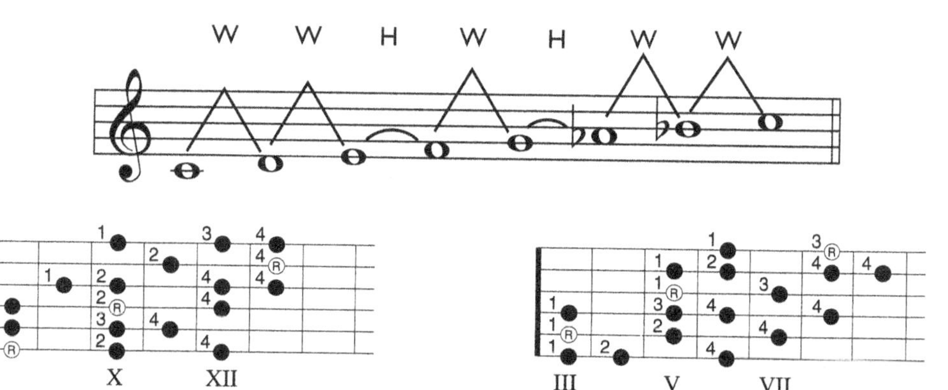

PHRYGIAN DOMINANT

Use the Phrygian dominant mode starting on the root of a 7♯5 chord. This does not work for the 9♯5 chord.

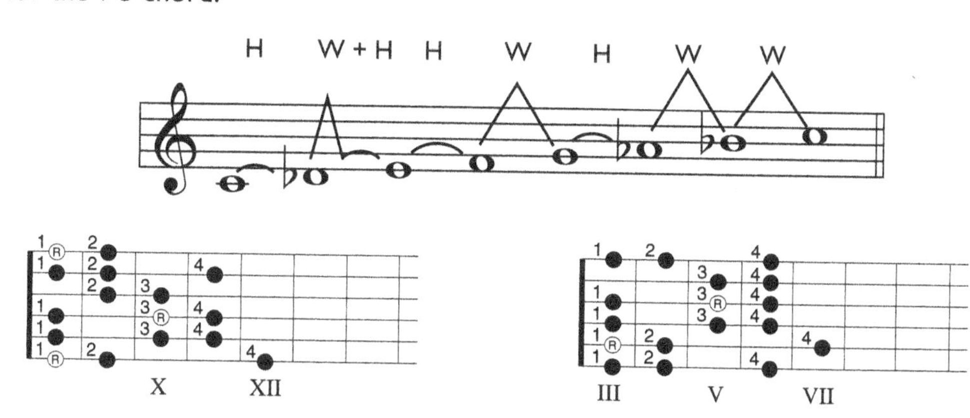

7♭9, 13♭9 and 7♯9 Chords

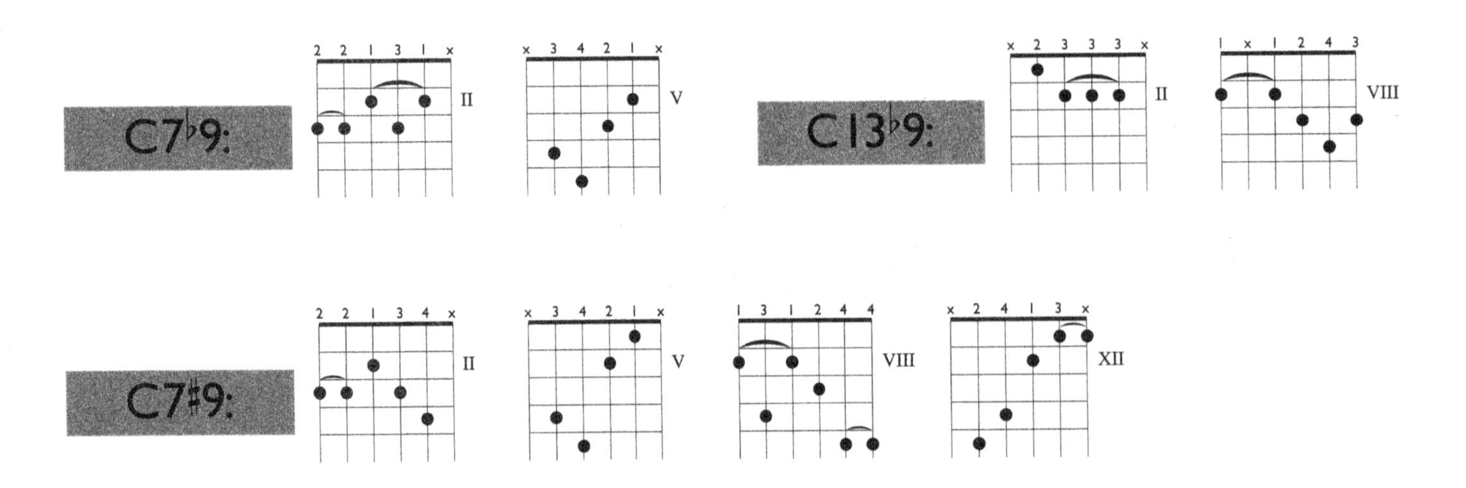

Chord and Scale Chart

Chords	Function	Major or Minor key	Scale or Mode	Starting on...
7♭9, 13♭9 and 7♯9 (*except where marked **)	Any	Both	Diminished	The 3rd of the chord
	Any	Both	Diminished	The 5th of the chord
	Any	Both	Diminished	The ♭7 of the chord
	Any	Both	Diminished	The ♭9 of the chord
	Any	Both	Diminished	½ step above the root of the chord
	Any	Both	Super Locrian	The root of the chord
	Any	Both	Phrygian Dominant*	The root of the chord
			**not good for a 7♯9 chord*	
7♯9	Any	Both	Minor Pentatonic	The root of the chord
	Any	Both	Blues	The root of the chord
	Any	Both	Dorian	The root of the chord

DIMINISHED

Use a diminished scale starting on the 3 of a 7♭9, 13♭9 or 7♯9 chord.

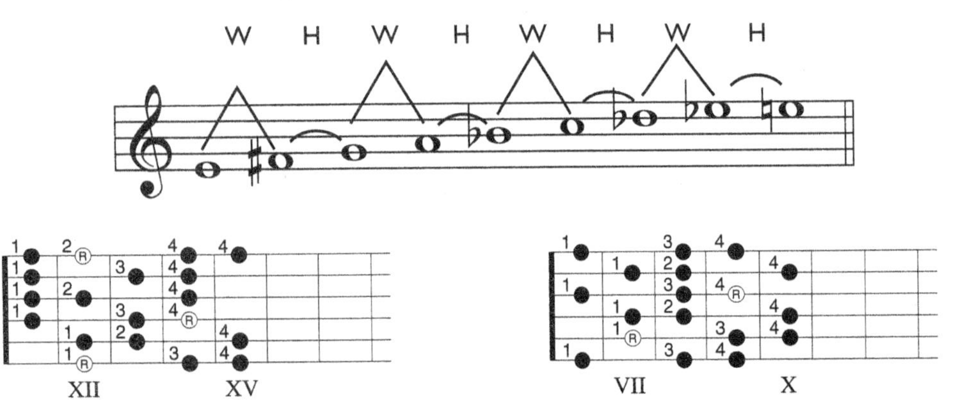

Use a diminished scale starting on the 5 of a 7♭9, 13♭9 or 7♯9 chord.

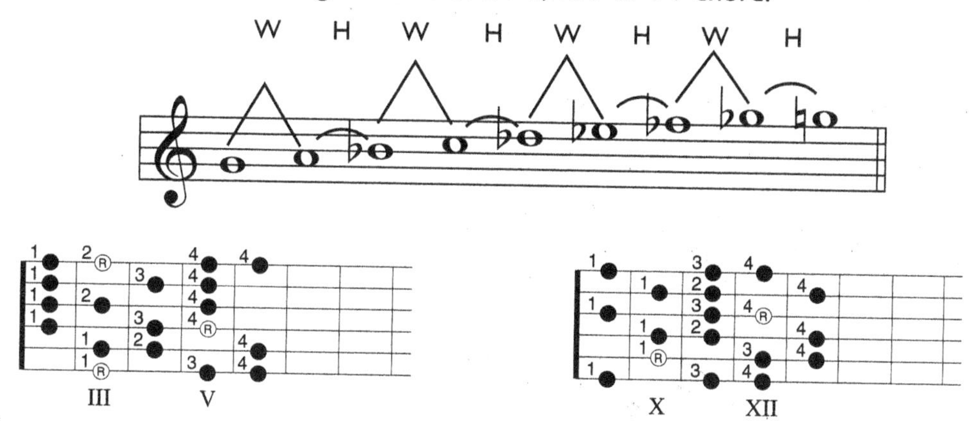

Use a diminished scale starting on the ♭7 of a 7♭9, 13♭9 or 7♯9 chord.

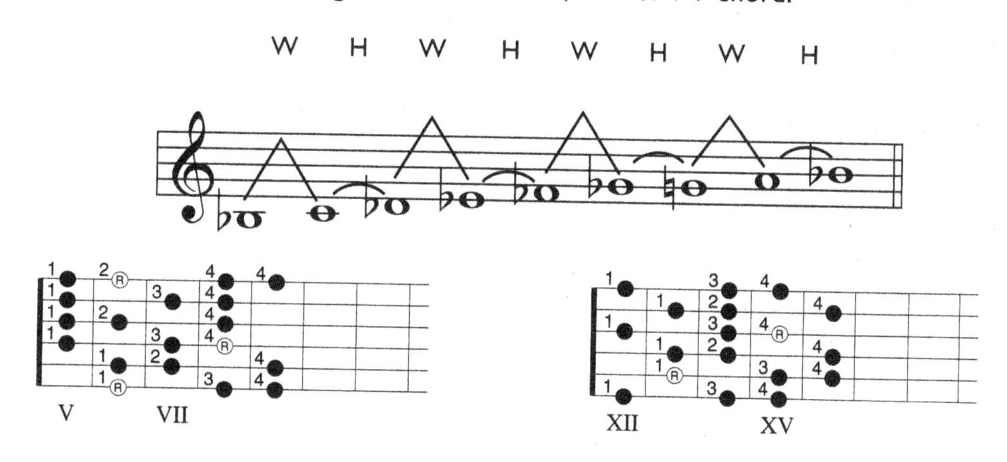

Use a diminished scale starting on the ♭9 or one half step above the root of a 7♭9, 13♭9 or 7♯9 chord.

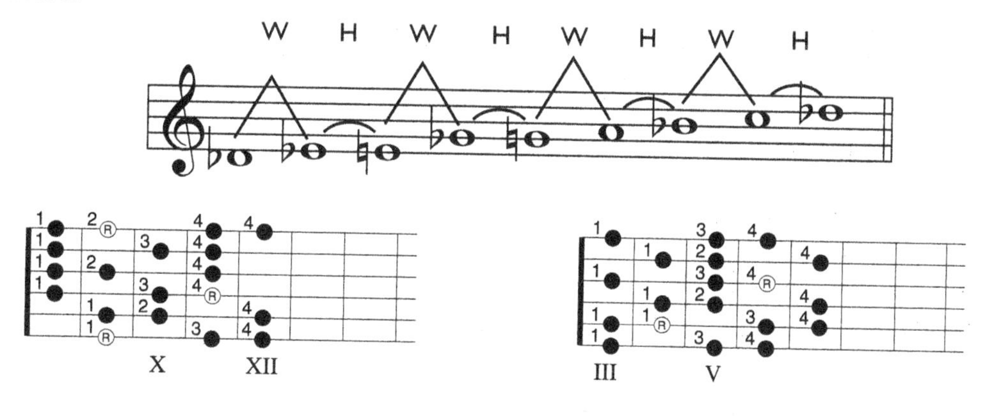

SUPER LOCRIAN

Use the super Locrian mode starting on the root of a $7^{\flat}9$, $13^{\flat}9$ or $7^{\sharp}9$ chord.

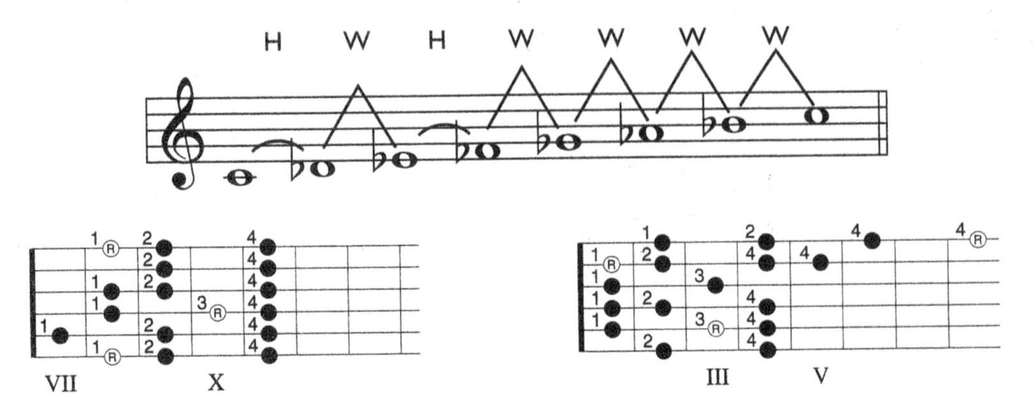

PHRYGIAN DOMINANT

Use the Phrygian dominant mode starting on the root of a $7^{\flat}9$ or $13^{\flat}9$ chord. This does not work for a $7^{\sharp}9$ chord.

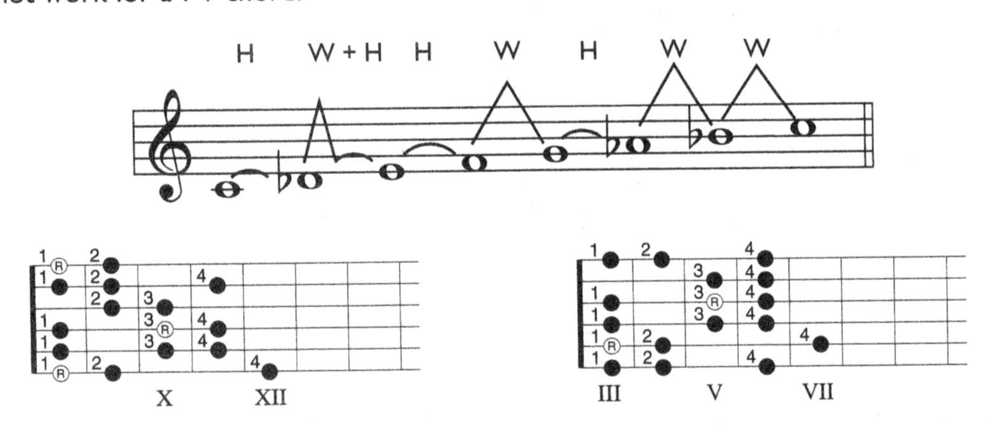

MINOR PENTATONIC

Use a minor pentatonic scale starting on the root of a $7^{\sharp}9$ chord.

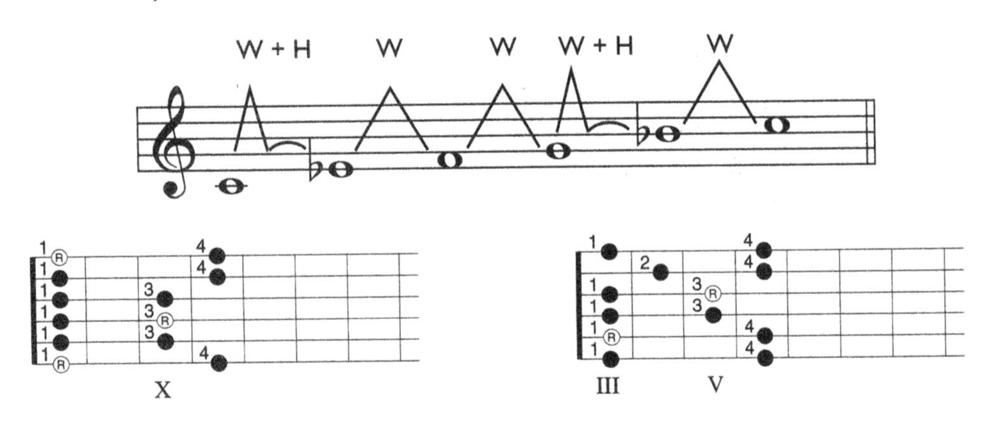

BLUES

Use a blues scale starting on the root of a 7♯9 chord.

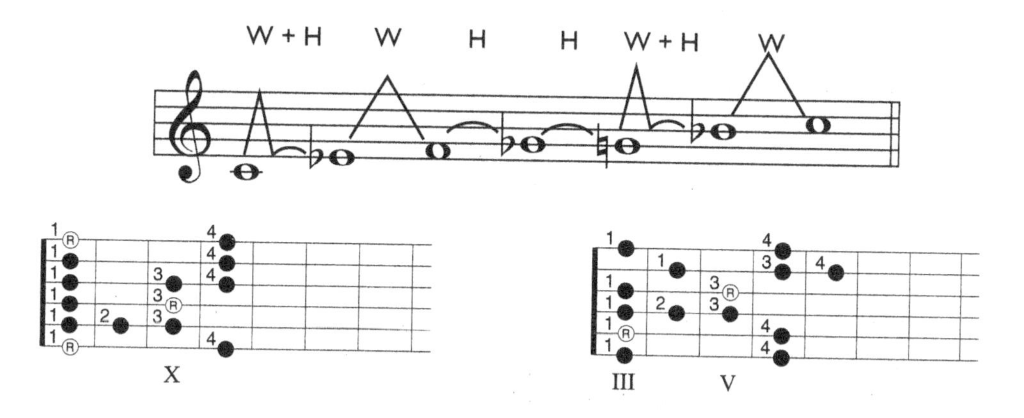

DORIAN

Use the Dorian mode starting on the root of a 7♯9 chord.

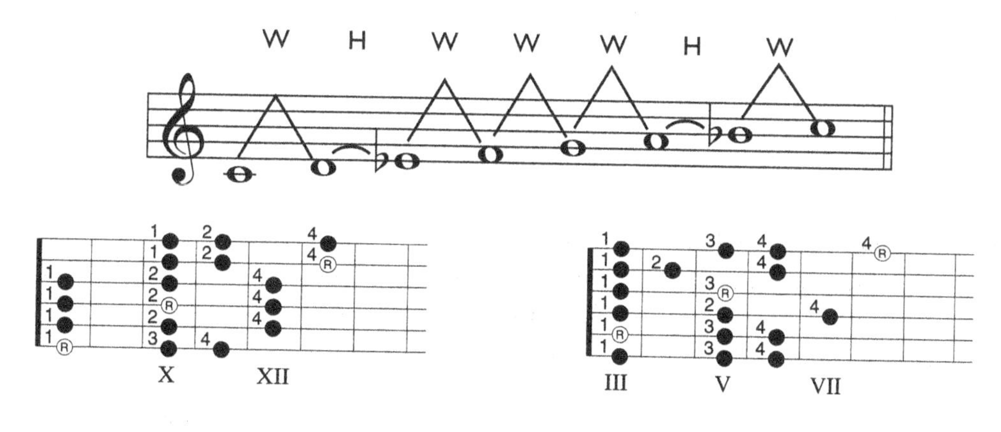

7♭5♭9, 7♭5#9, 13#9#11 and 7#5#9 Chords

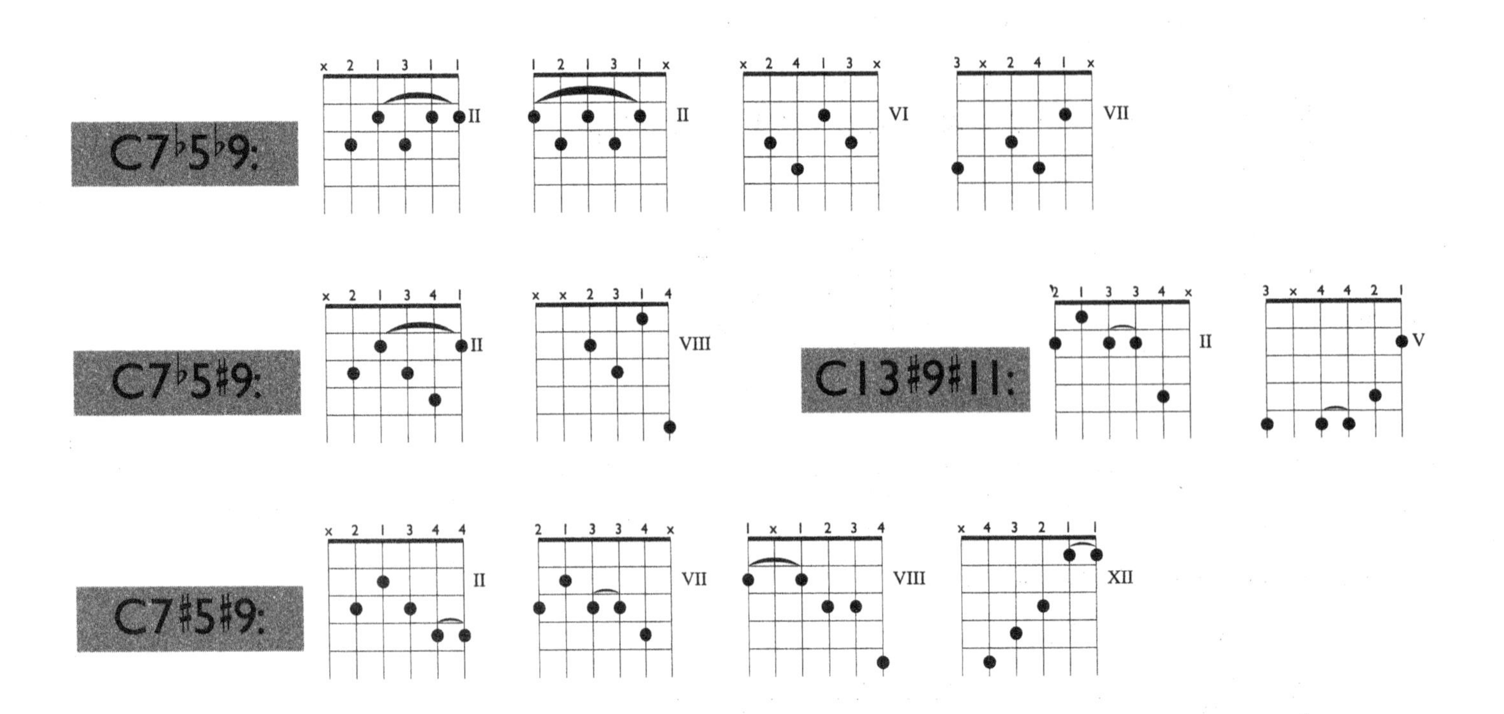

Chord and Scale Chart

Chords	Function	Major or Minor key	Scale or Mode	Starting on...
7♭5♭9, 7♭5#9 and 13#9#11	Any	Both	Diminished	½ step above the root of the chord
	Any	Both	Diminished	The 3 of the chord
	Any	Both	Diminished	The ♭7 of the chord
	Any	Both	Diminished	The ♭9 of the chord
	Any	Both	Super Locrian	The root of the chord
7♭5♭9	Any	Both	Major Pentatonic	½ step above the root of the chord
7♭5#9 and 13#9#11	Any	Both	Blues	The root of the chord
7#5#9	Any	Both	Super Locrian	The root of the chord

DIMINISHED

Use a diminished scale starting on the 3 of a 7♭5♭9, 7♭5#9 or 13#9#11 chord.

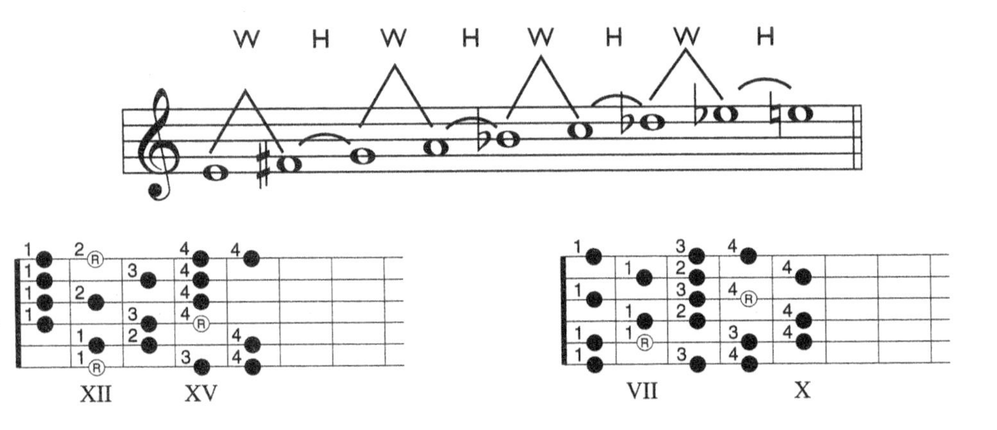

Use a diminished scale starting on the $^{\flat}7$ of a $7^{\flat}5^{\flat}9$, $7^{\flat}5^{\sharp}9$ or $13^{\sharp}9^{\sharp}11$ chord.

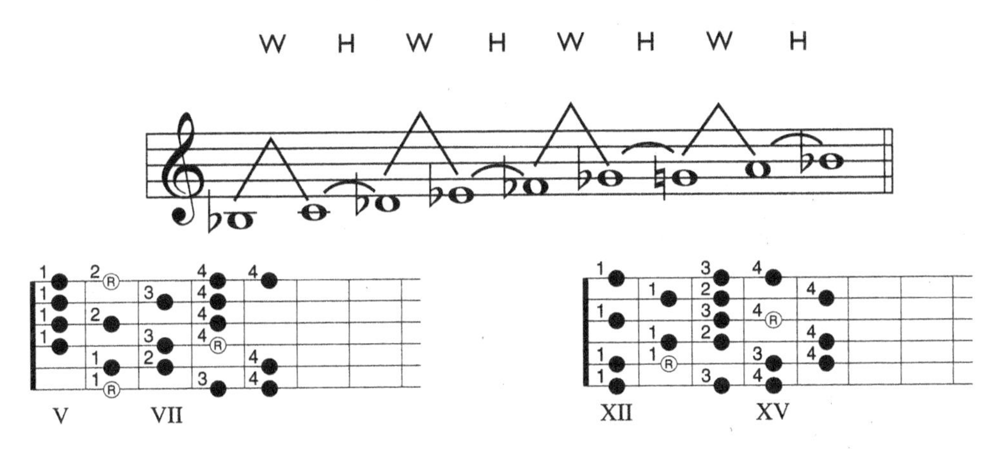

Use a diminished scale starting one half step above the root of a $7^{\flat}5^{\flat}9$, $7^{\flat}5^{\sharp}9$ or $13^{\sharp}9^{\sharp}11$ chord.

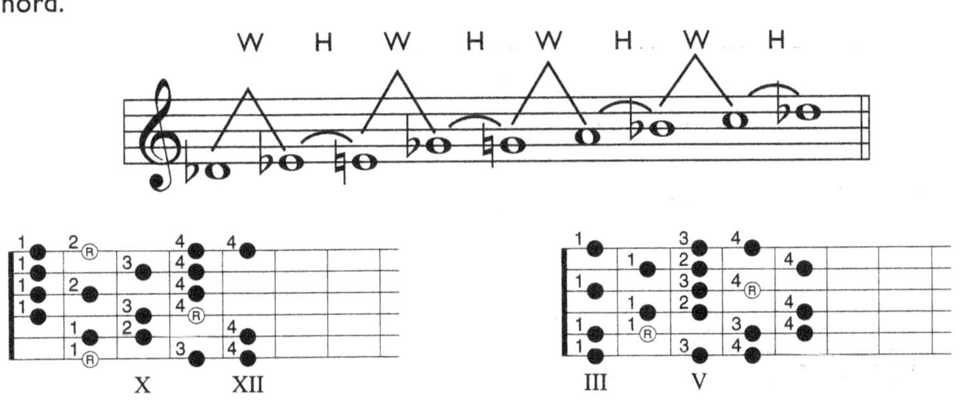

SUPER LOCRIAN

Use the super Locrian mode starting on the root of a $7^{\flat}5^{\flat}9$, $7^{\flat}5^{\sharp}9$, $13^{\sharp}9^{\sharp}11$ or $7^{\sharp}5^{\sharp}9$ chord.

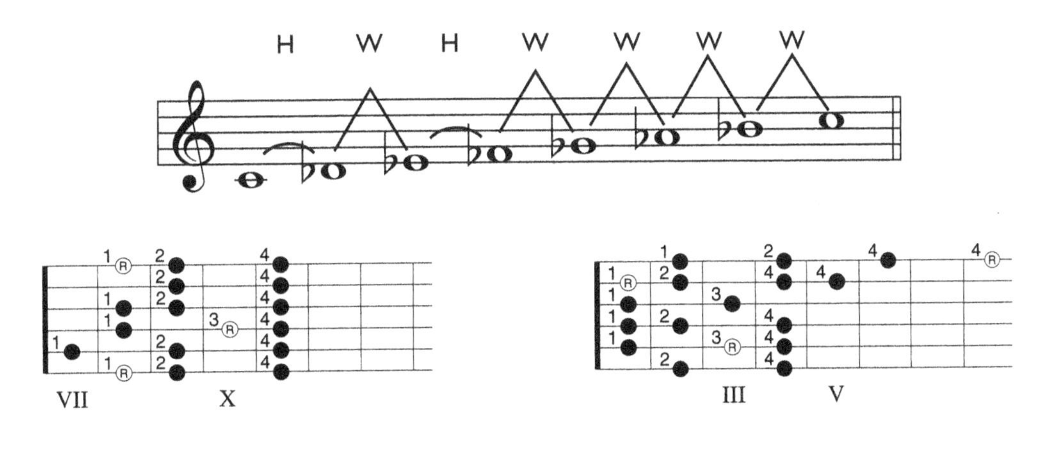

MAJOR PENTATONIC

Use a major pentatonic scale starting one half step above the root of a $7^{\flat}5^{\flat}9$ chord.

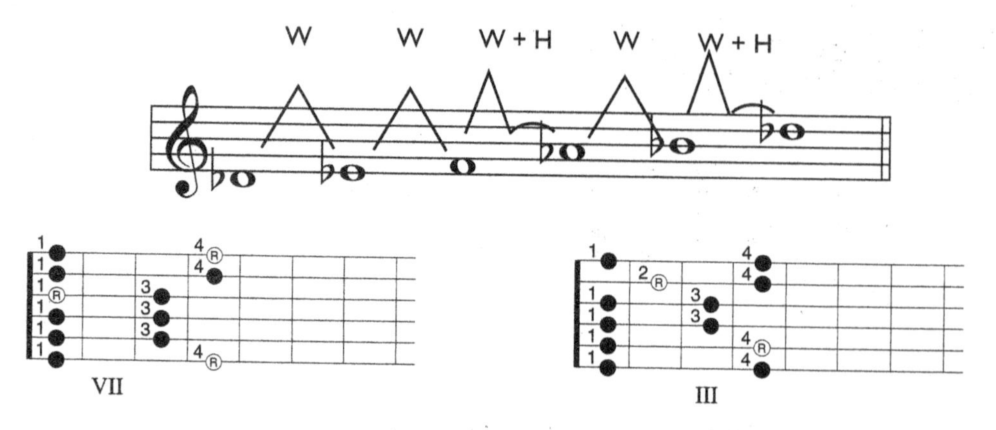

BLUES

Use a blues scale starting from the root of a $7^{\flat}5^{\sharp}9$ or $13^{\sharp}9^{\sharp}11$ chord.

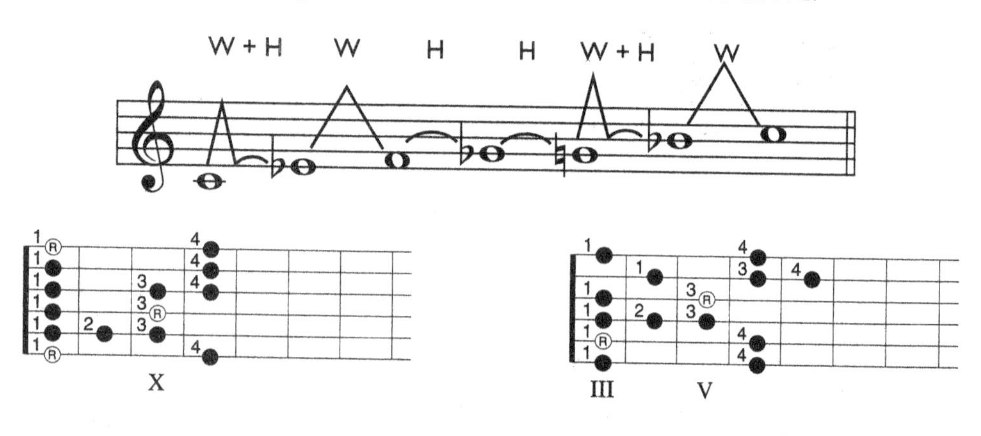

7♯5♭9 Chords

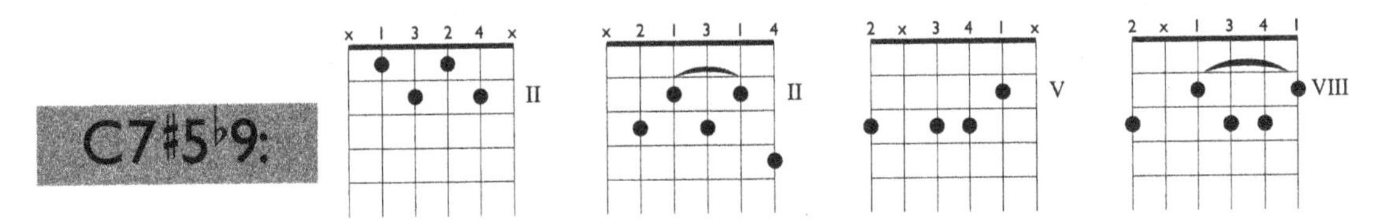

Chord and Scale Chart

Chords	Function	Major or Minor key	Scale or Mode	Starting on...
7♯5♭9	Any	Both	Super Locrian	The root of the chord
	Any	Both	Phrygian Dominant	The root of the chord

SUPER LOCRIAN

Use the super Locrian mode starting on the root of a 7♯5♭9 chord.

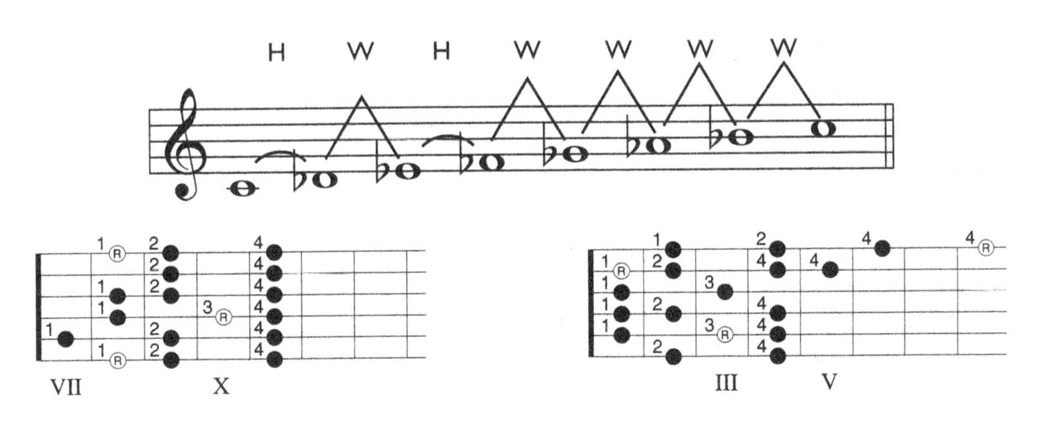

PHRYGIAN DOMINANT

Use the Phrygian dominant mode starting on the root of a 7♯5♭9 chord.

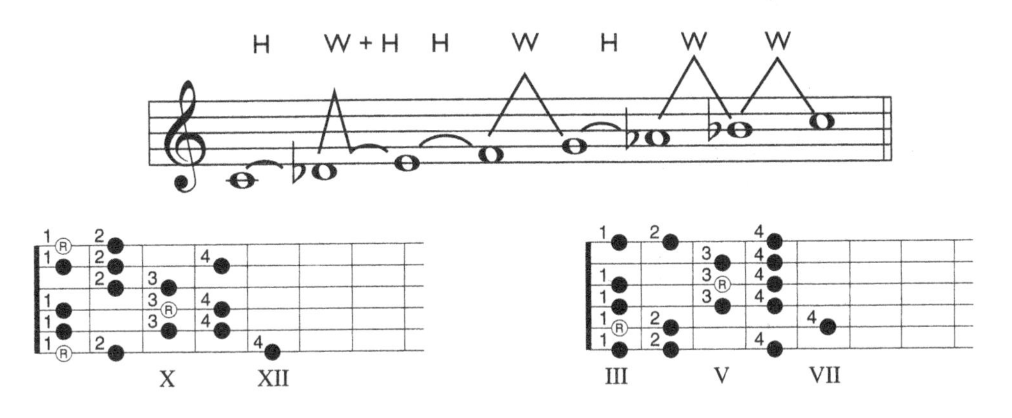

9♯11 and 13♯11 Chords

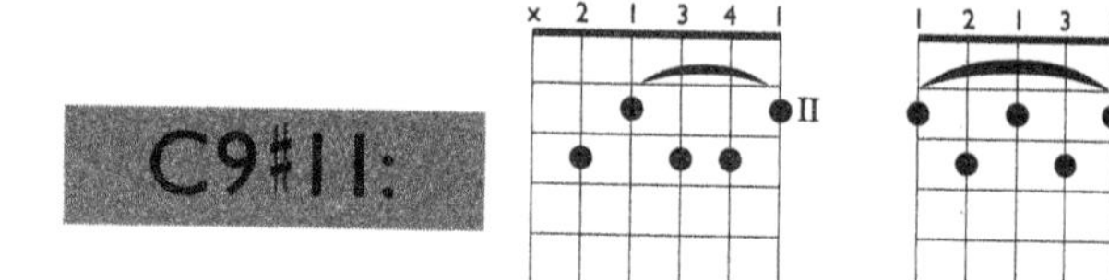

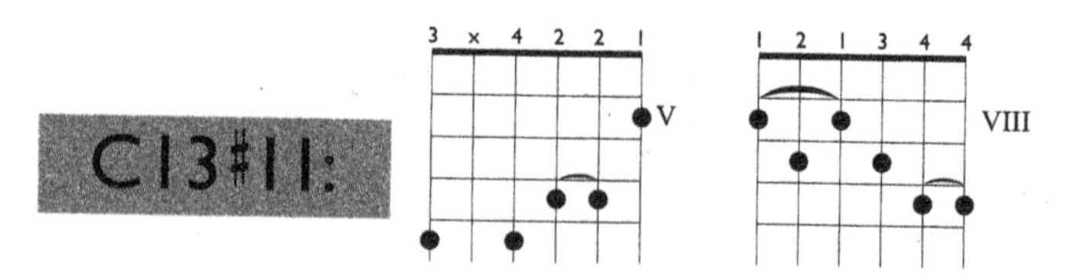

Chord and Scale Chart

Chords	Function	Major or Minor key	Scale or Mode	Starting on...
9♯11 and 13♯11	Any	Both	Lydian ♭7	The root of the chord
	Any	Both	Blues	The root of the chord

LYDIAN ♭7

Use the Lydian ♭7 mode starting on the root of a 9♯11 or 13♯11 chord.

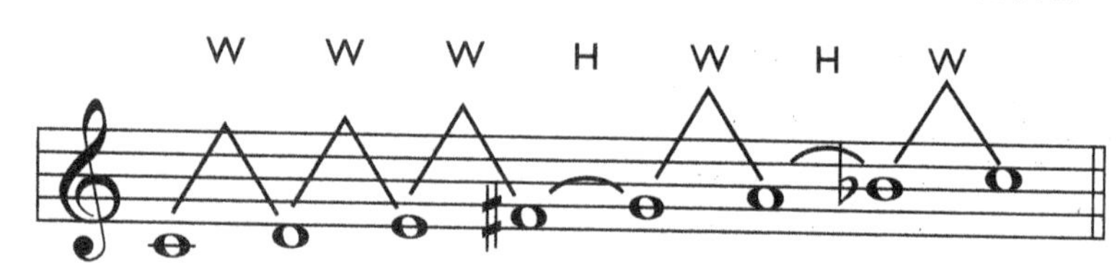

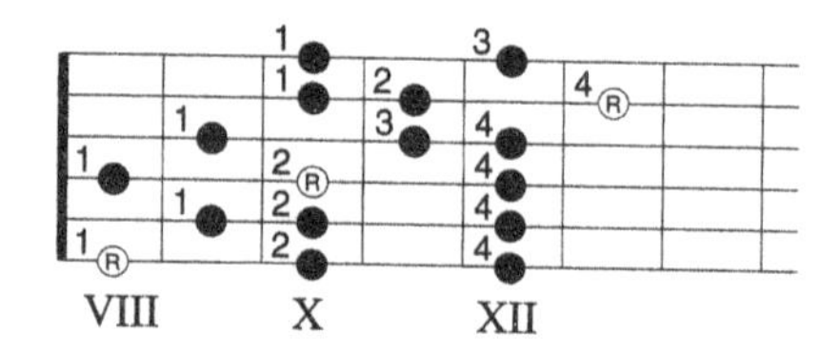

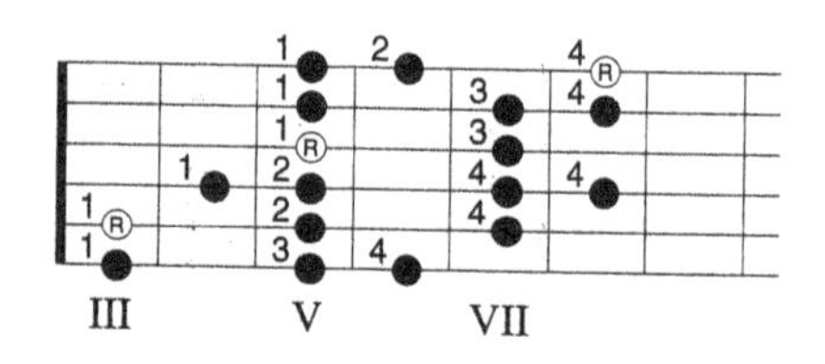

BLUES

Use a blues scale starting on the root of a 9♯11 or 13♯11 chord.

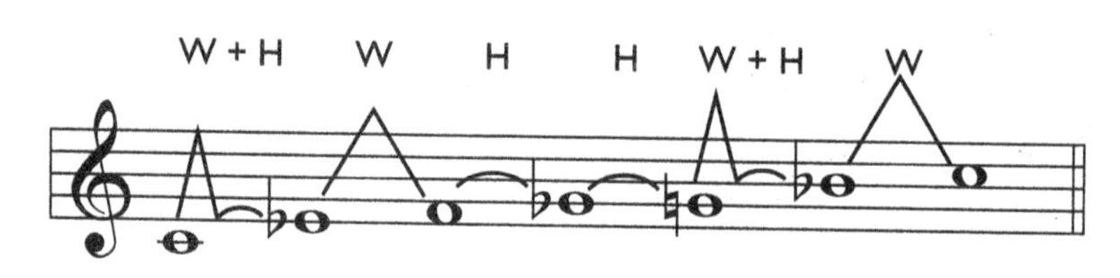

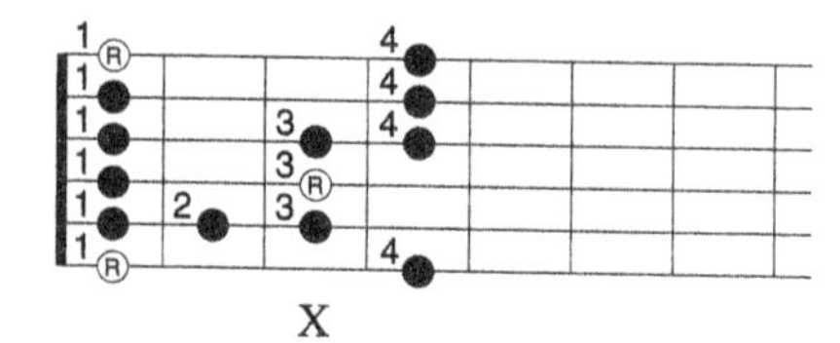

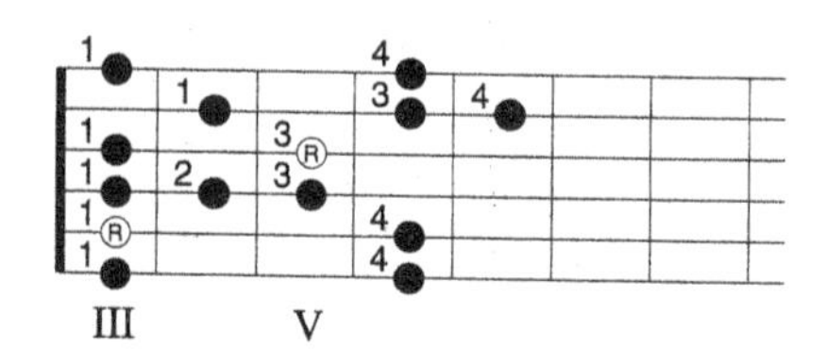

AUGMENTED TRIADS

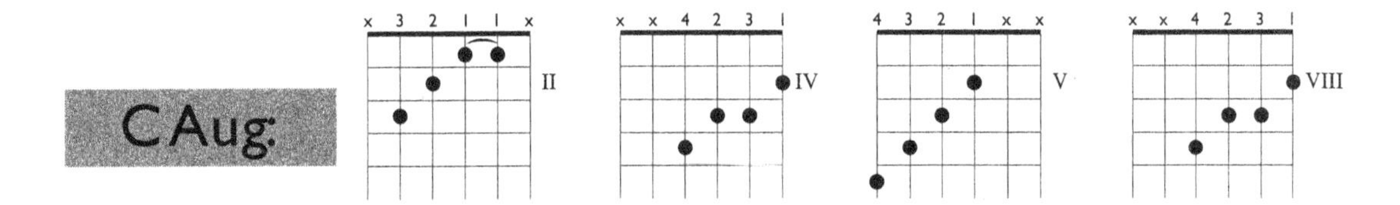

Chord	Function	Major or Minor key	Scale or Mode	Starting on...
Aug	Any	Both	Whole Tone	The root of the chord
	Any	Both	Whole Tone	The 3 of the chord
	Any	Both	Whole Tone	The ♯5 of the chord

WHOLE TONE

Use a whole tone scale starting on the root of an augmented triad (aug).

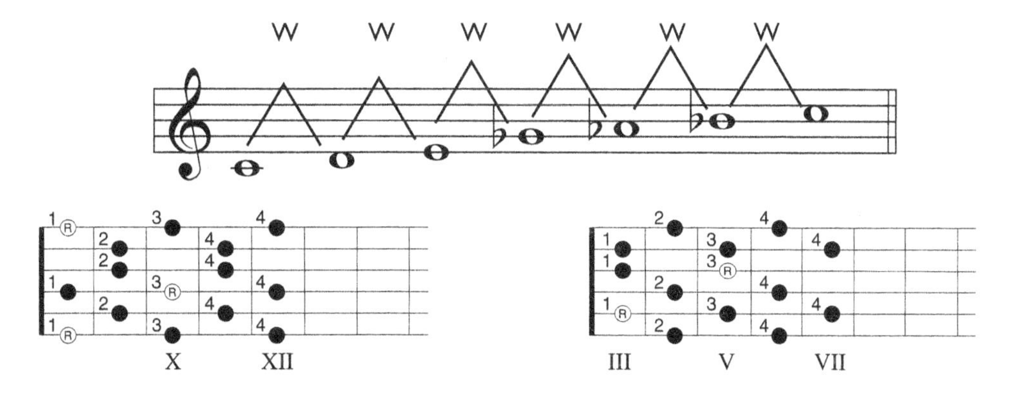

You can also use a whole tone scale starting on the 3rd of an augmented triad (aug).

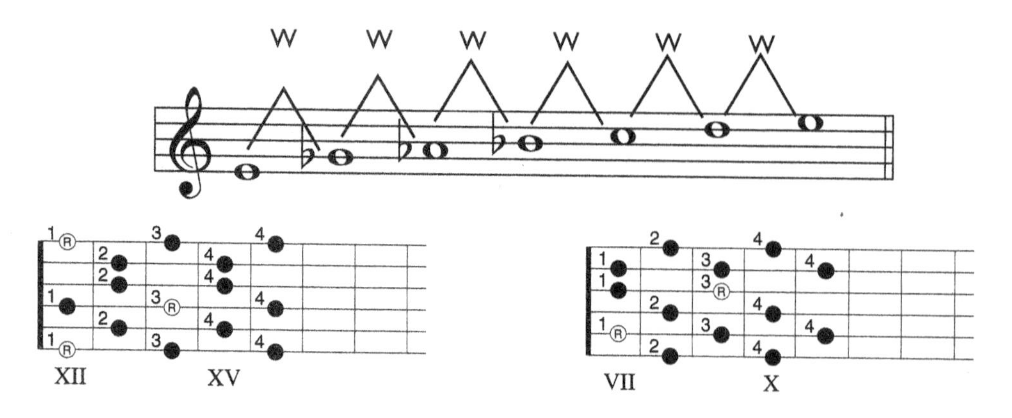

Use a whole tone scale starting on the ♯5 of an augmented triad.

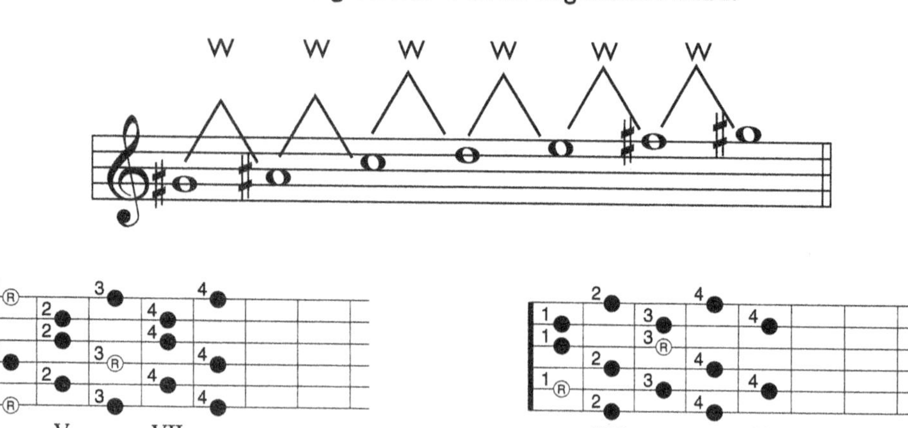

MINOR CHORDS

Minor Triads

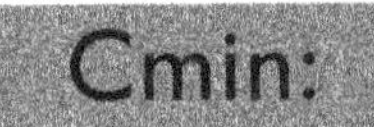

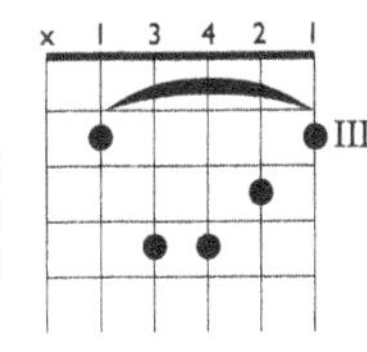

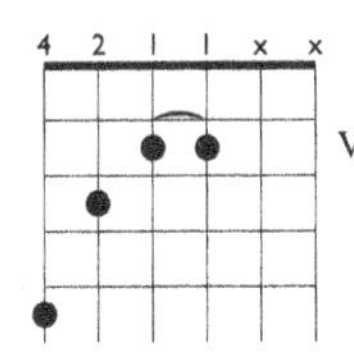

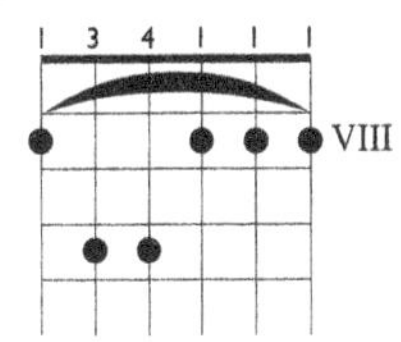

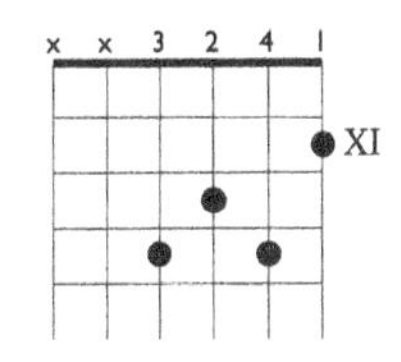

Chord and Scale Chart

Chord	Function	Major or Minor key	Scale or Mode	Starting on...
Minor triads (min)	i	Minor	Natural Minor (Aeolian)	The root of the chord
	vi	Major		
	i	Minor	Harmonic Minor	The root of the chord
	i	Minor	Melodic Minor	The root of the chord
	i or ii	Minor	Minor Pentatonic	The root of the chord
	ii, iii or vi	Major		
	ii	Major	Dorian	The root of the chord
	ii	Minor	Dorian ♭2	The root of the chord
	iii	Major	Phrygian	The root of the chord
	iv	Minor	Lydian ♭3♭7	The root of the chord

NATURAL MINOR (AEOLIAN)

Use a natural minor scale starting on the root of a minor triad when it functions as i in a minor key or vi in a major key.

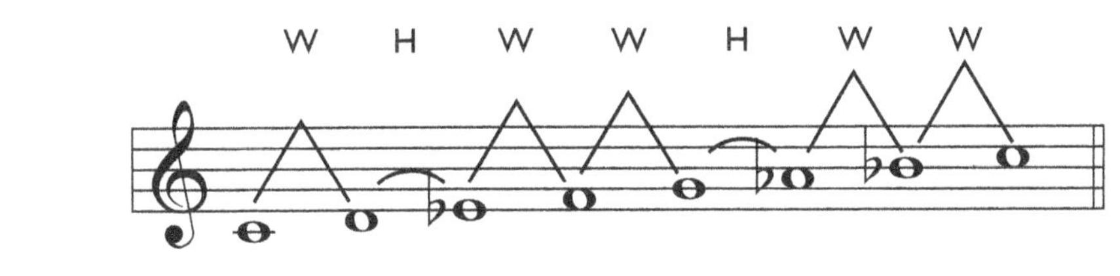

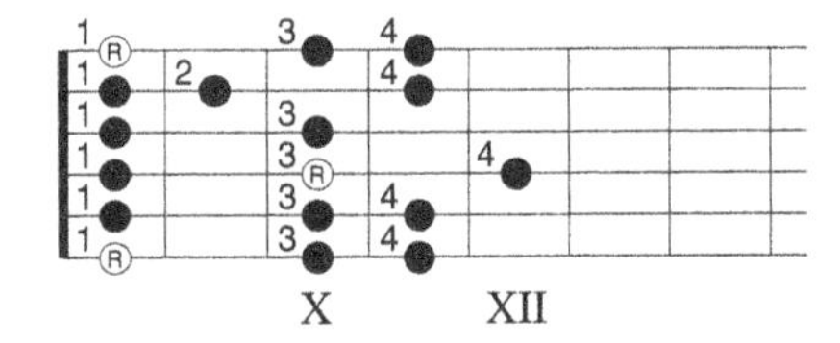

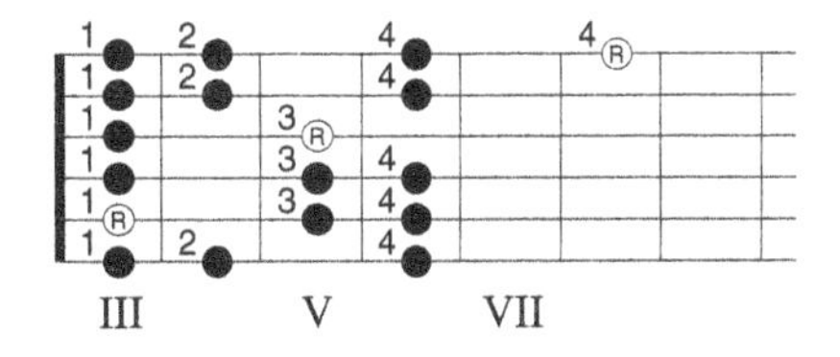

HARMONIC MINOR

Use a harmonic minor scale starting on the root of a minor triad when it functions as i in a minor key.

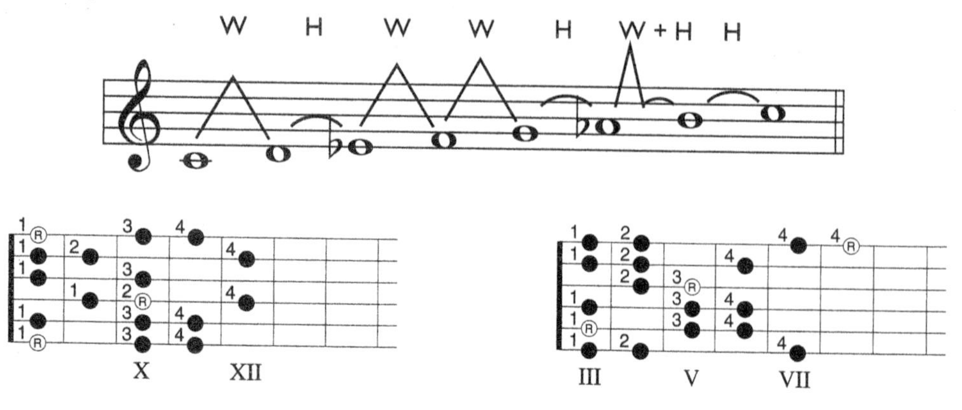

MELODIC MINOR

Use a melodic minor scale starting on the root of a minor triad when it functions as i in a minor key.

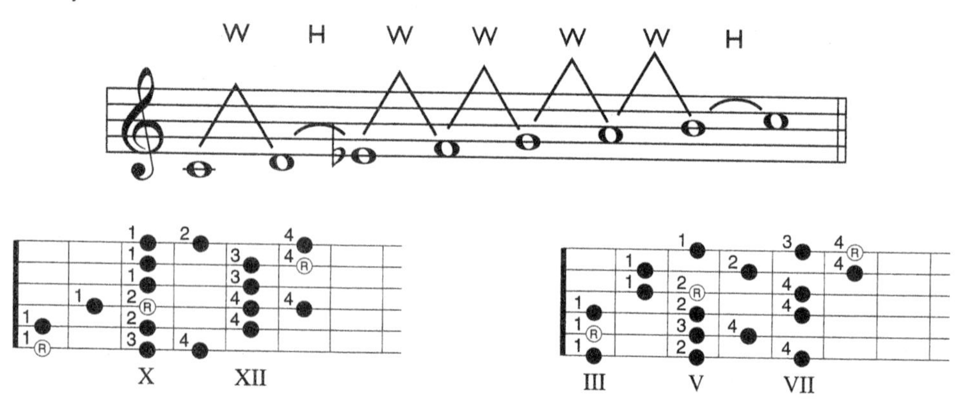

MINOR PENTATONIC

Use a minor pentatonic scale starting on the root of a minor triad when it functions as i or ii in a minor key; or when it functions as ii, iii or vi in a major key.

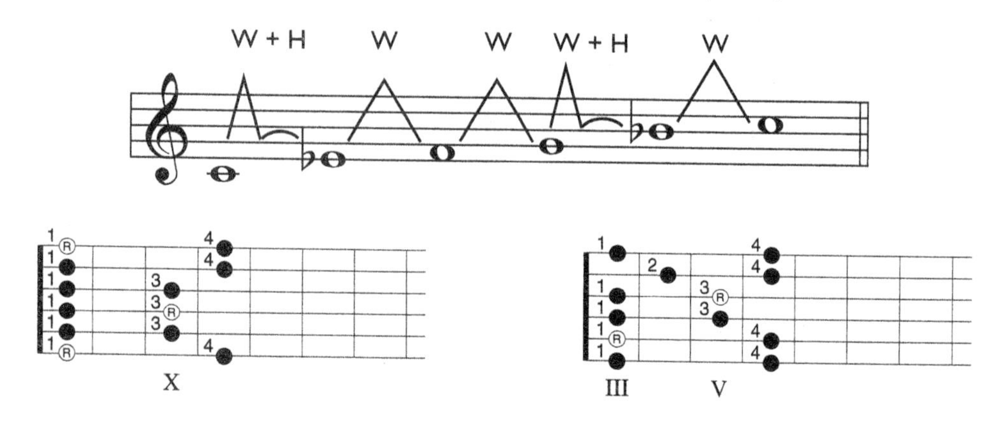

DORIAN

Use the Dorian mode starting on the root of a minor triad when it functions as ii in a major key.

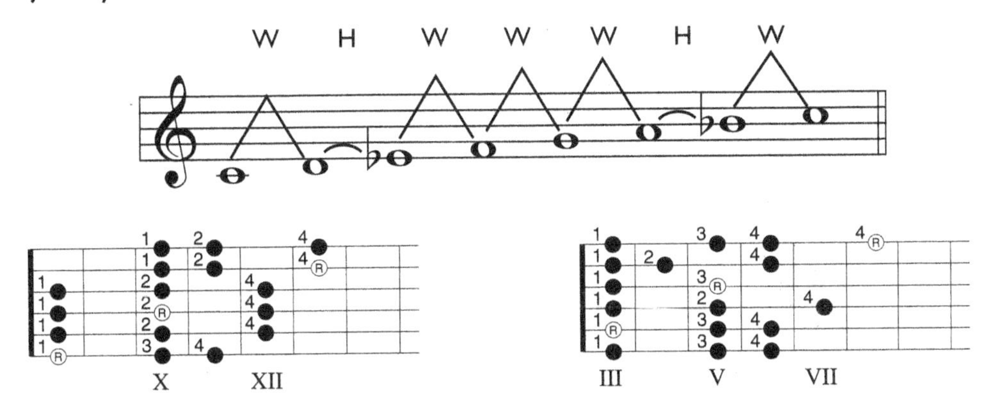

DORIAN $\flat$2

Use the Dorian $\flat$2 mode starting on the root of a minor triad when it functions as ii in a minor key.

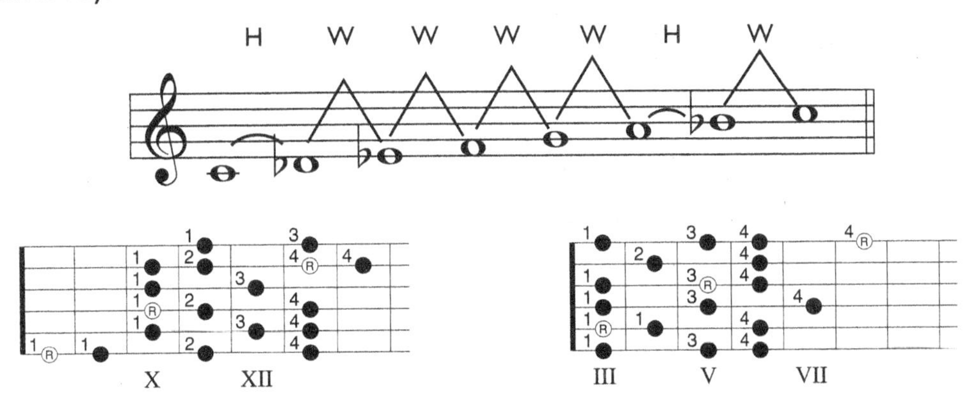

PHRYGIAN

Use the Phrygian mode starting on the root of a minor triad when it functions as iii in a major key.

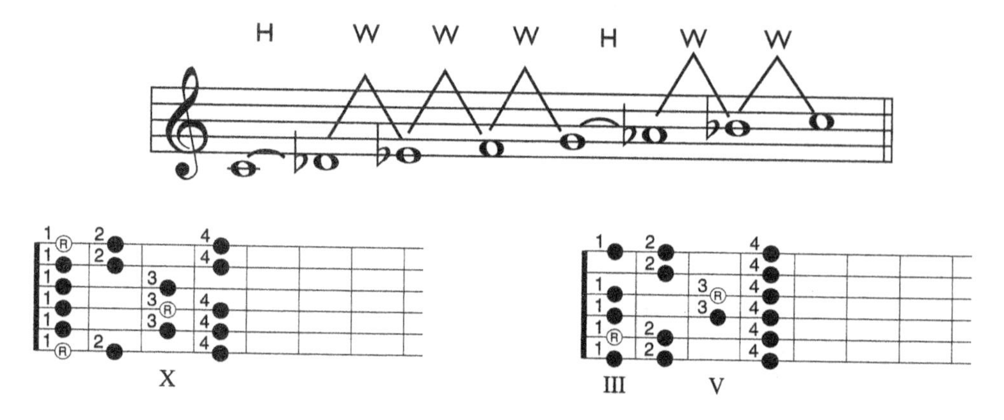

LYDIAN ♭3♭7

Use the Lydian ♭3♭7 mode starting on the root of a minor triad when it functions as iv in a minor key.

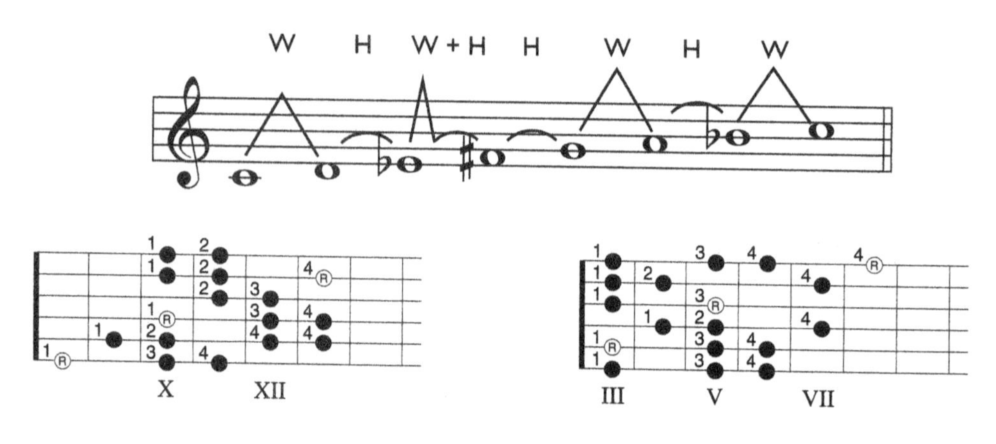

PHRYGIAN

Use the Phrygian mode starting on the root of a minor triad when it functions as iii in a major key.

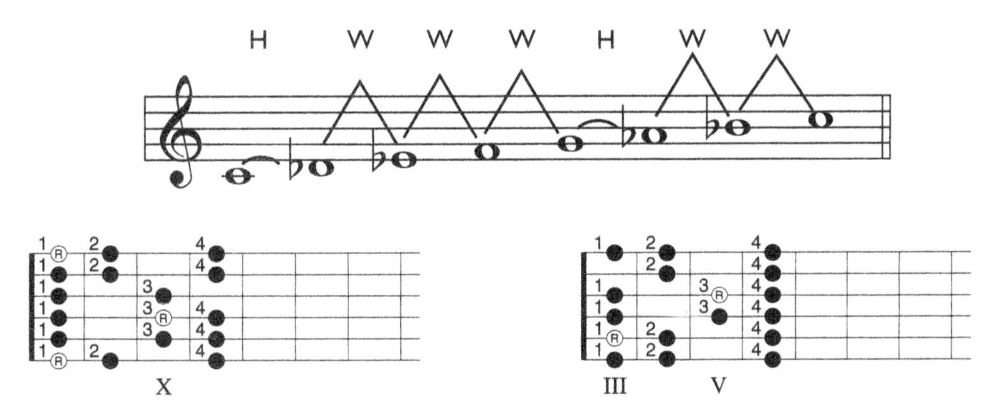

LYDIAN ♭3♭7

Use the Lydian ♭3♭7 mode starting on the root of a minor triad when it functions as iv in a minor key.

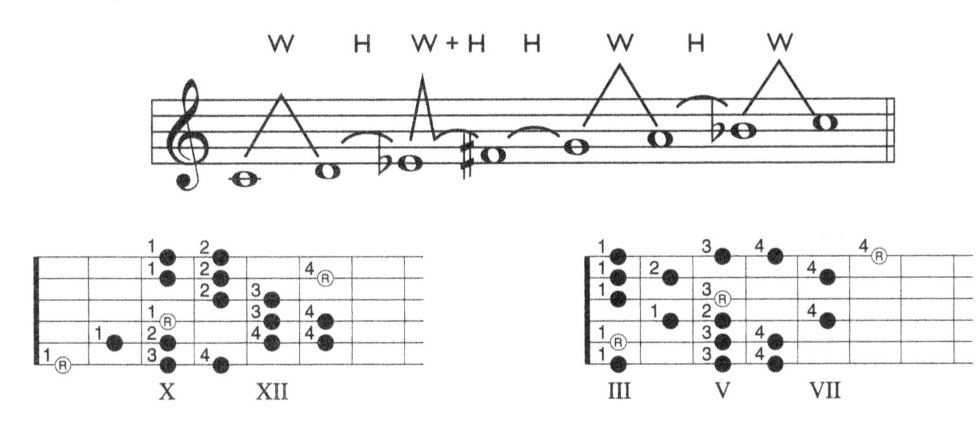

DORIAN ♭2

Use the Dorian ♭2 mode starting on the root of a min6 chord when it functions as ii in a minor key.

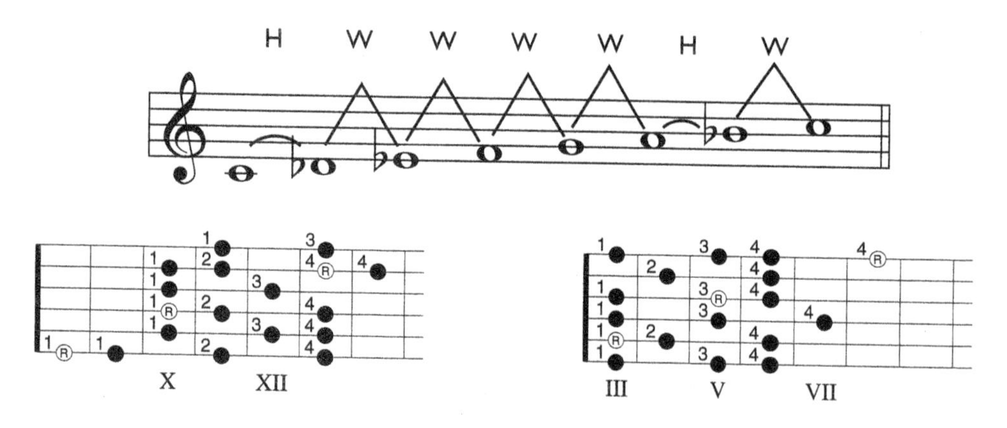

DORIAN

Use the Dorian mode starting on the root of a min6 chord when it functions as ii in a major key.

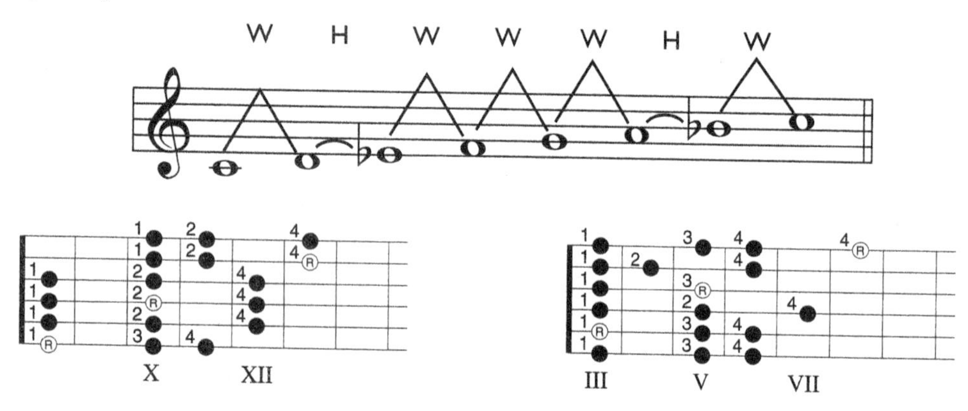

LYDIAN ♭3♭7

Use the Lydian ♭3♭7 mode starting on the root of a min6 chord when it functions iv in a minor key.

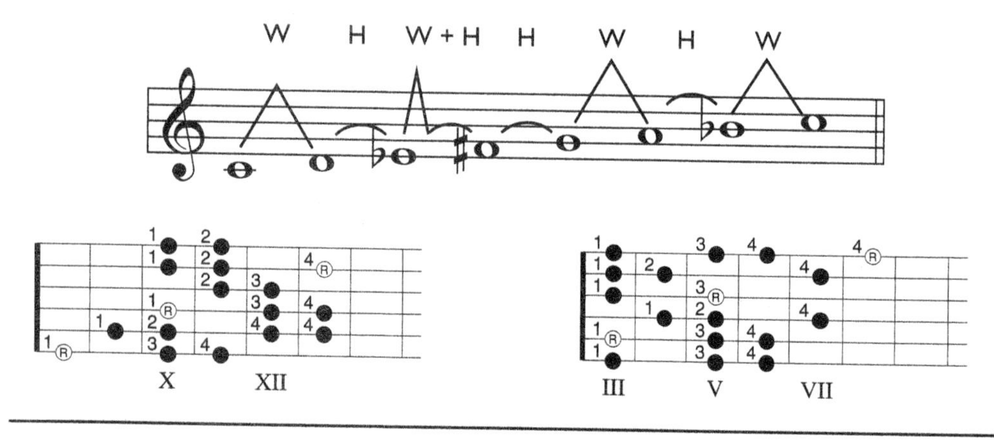

min7 Chords

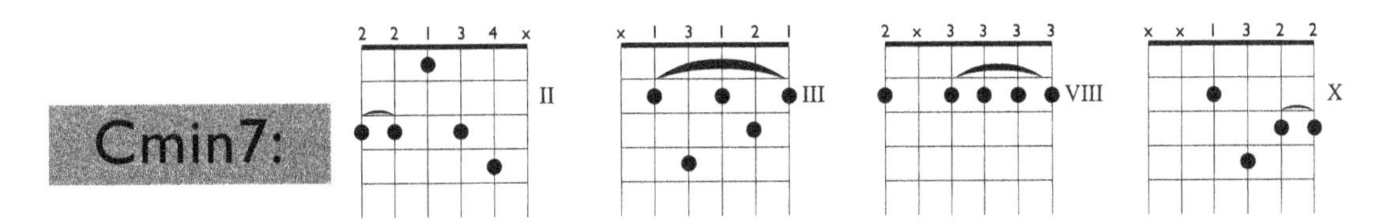

Chord and Scale Chart

Chord	Function	Major or Minor key	Scale or Mode	Starting on...
min7	ii, iii or vi	Major	Minor Pentatonic	The root of the chord
	ii	Minor		
	ii	Minor	Dorian ♭2	The root of the chord
	ii	Major	Dorian	The root of the chord
	iii	Major	Phrygian	The root of the chord
	iv	Minor	Lydian ♭3♭7	The root of the chord
	vi	Minor	Natural Minor (Aeolian)	The root of the chord

MINOR PENTATONIC

Use a minor pentatonic scale starting on the root of a min7 chord when it functions as ii in a minor key, or when it functions as ii, iii or vi in a major key.

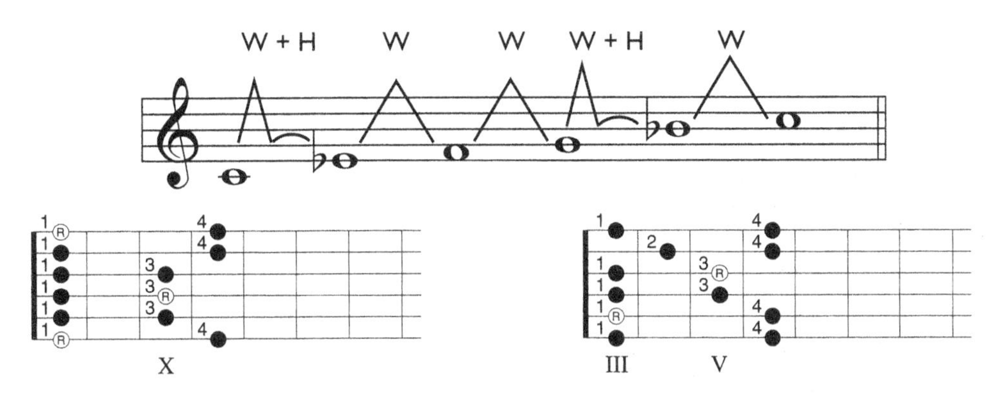

DORIAN ♭2

Use the Dorian ♭2 mode starting on the root of a min7 chord when it functions as ii in a minor key.

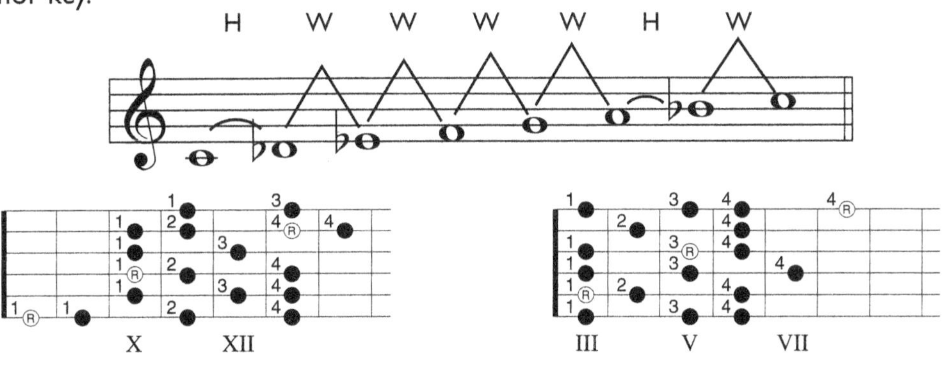

DORIAN

Use the Dorian mode starting on the root of a min7 chord when it functions as ii in a major key.

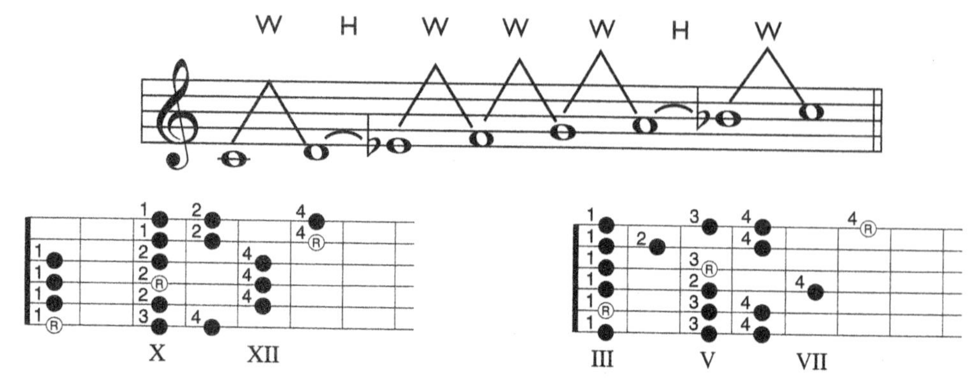

PHRYGIAN

Use the Phrygian mode starting on the root of a min7 chord when it functions as iii in a major key.

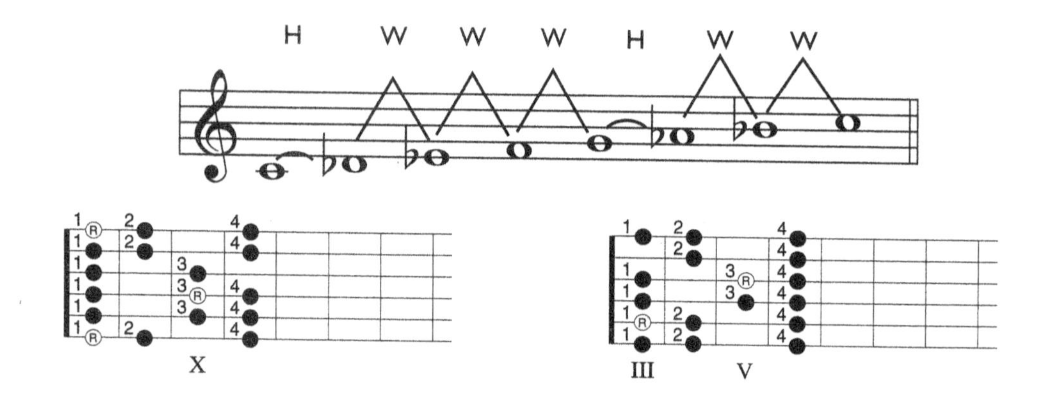

LYDIAN ♭3♭7

Use the Lydian♭3♭7 mode starting on the root of a min7 chord when it functions as iv in a minor key.

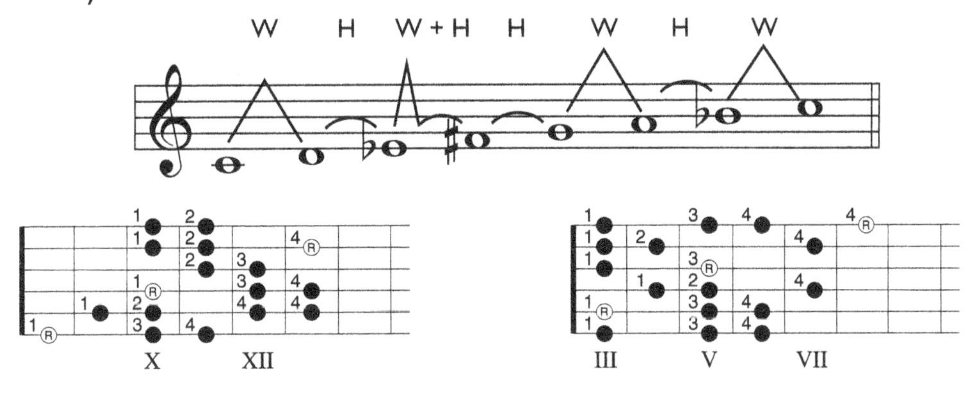

NATURAL MINOR (AEOLIAN)

Use the natural minor scale (Aeolian mode) starting on the root of a min7 chord when it functions as vi in a major key.

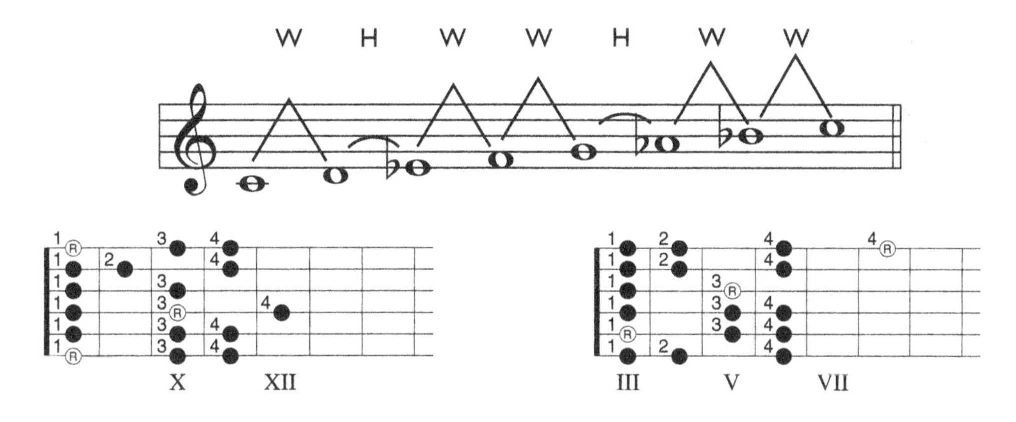

min9 Chords

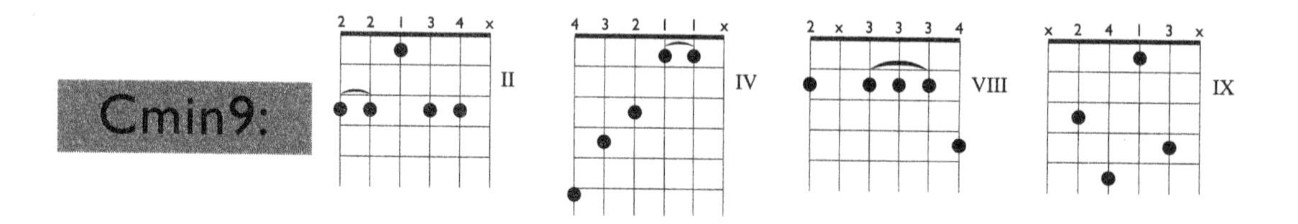

Chord and Scale Chart

Chord	Function	Major or Minor key	Scale or Mode	Starting on...
min9	ii or vi	Major	Minor Pentatonic	The root of the chord
	ii	Major	Dorian	The root of the chord
	iv	Minor	Lydian ♭3♭7	The root of the chord
	vi	Major	Natural Minor (Aeolian)	The root of the chord

MINOR PENTATONIC

Use a minor pentatonic scale starting on the root of a min9 chord when it functions as ii or vi in a major key.

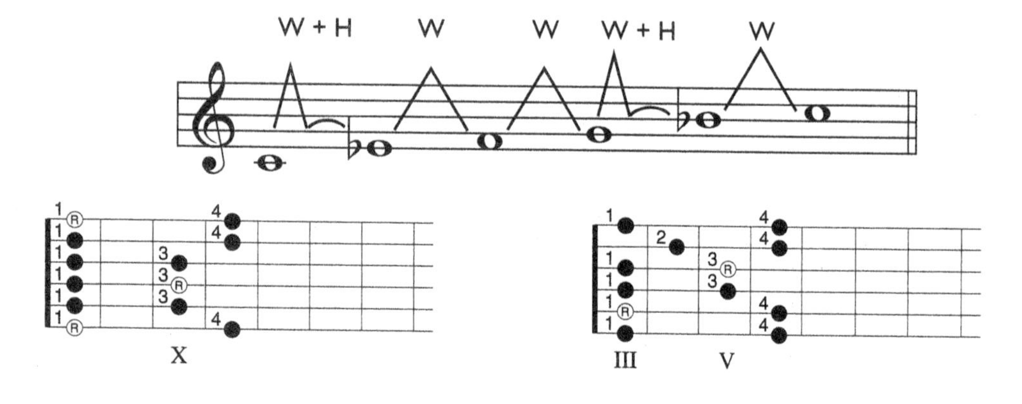

DORIAN

Use the Dorian mode starting on the root of a min9 chord when it functions as ii in a major key.

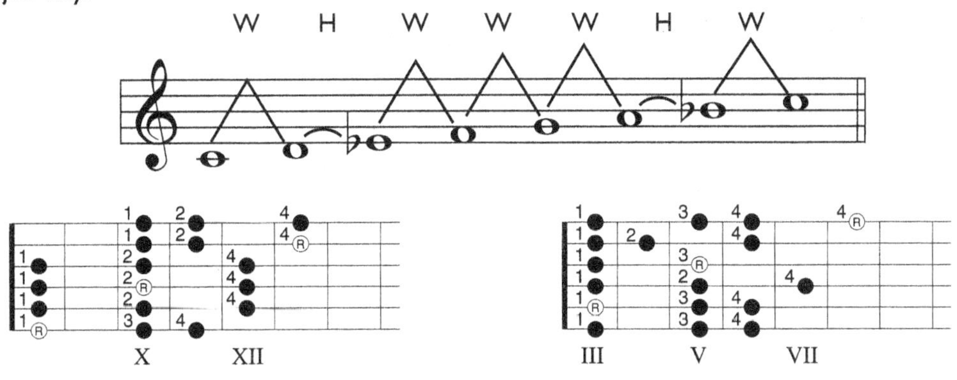

LYDIAN ♭3♭7

Use the Lydian ♭3♭7 mode starting on the root of a min9 when it functions as iv in a minor key.

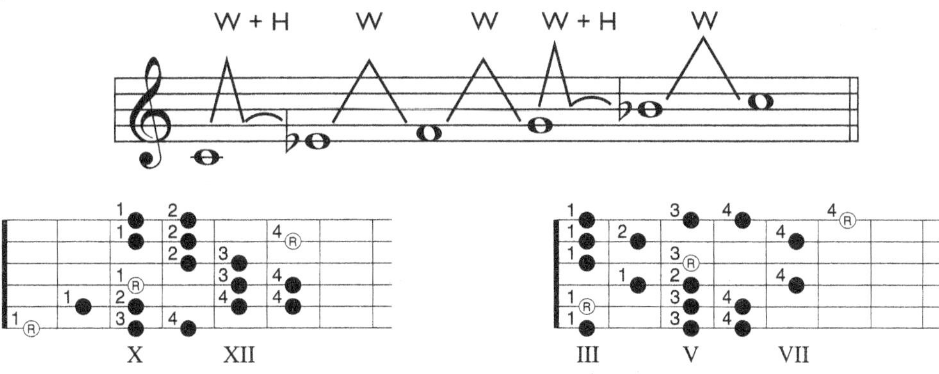

NATURAL MINOR (AEOLIAN)

Use a natural minor scale (Aeolian mode) starting on the root of a min9 chord when it functions as vi in a major key.

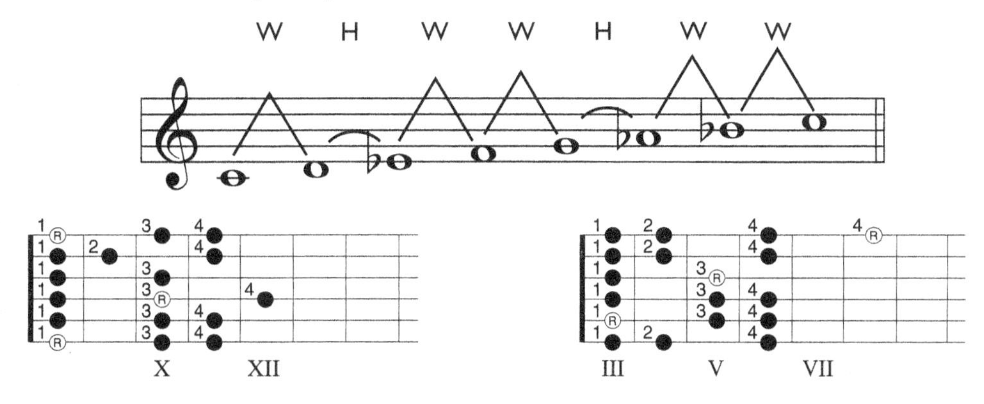

min11 Chords

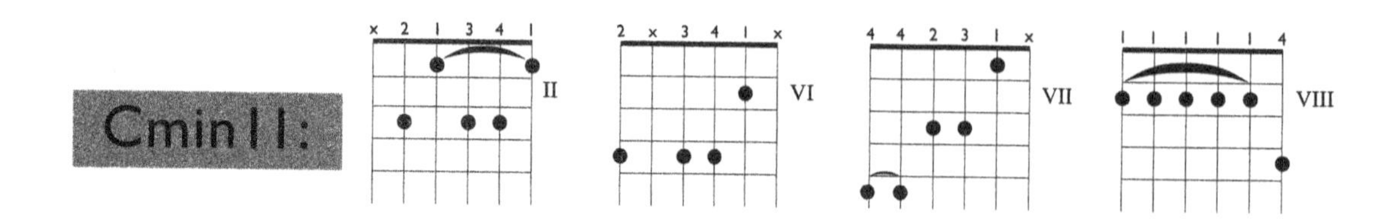

Chord and Scale Chart

Chord	Function	Major or Minor key	Scale or Mode	Starting on...
min11 *except where marked	ii	Minor	Minor Pentatonic	The root of the chord
	ii or iii	Major	Minor Pentatonic	The root of the chord
	ii	Major	Dorian	The root of the chord
	ii	Minor	Dorian ♭2* *when the 9th is not present	The root of the chord
	iii	Major	Phrygian* *when the 9th is not present	The root of the chord
	iv	Minor	Lydian ♭3♭7	The root of the chord
	vi	Major	Natural Minor (Aeolian)	The root of the chord

MINOR PENTATONIC

Use a minor pentatonic scale starting on the root of a min11 chord when it functions as ii in a minor key, or ii or iii in a major key.

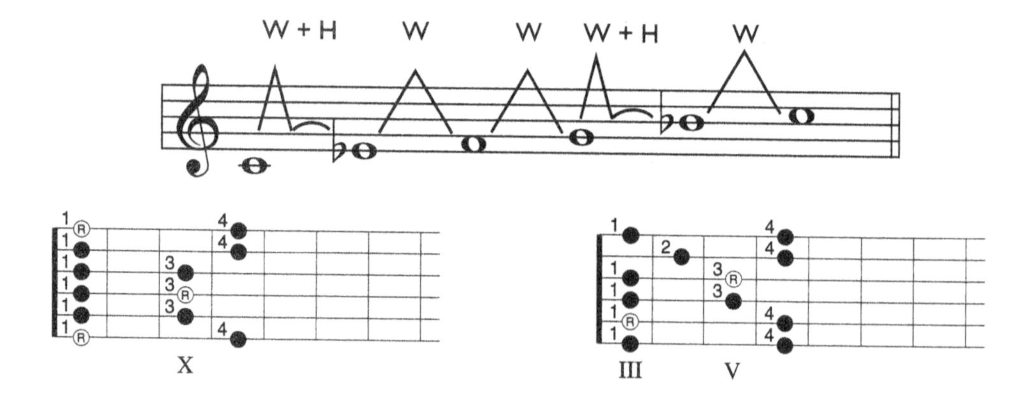

DORIAN

Use the Dorian mode starting on the root of a min11 chord when it functions as ii in a major key.

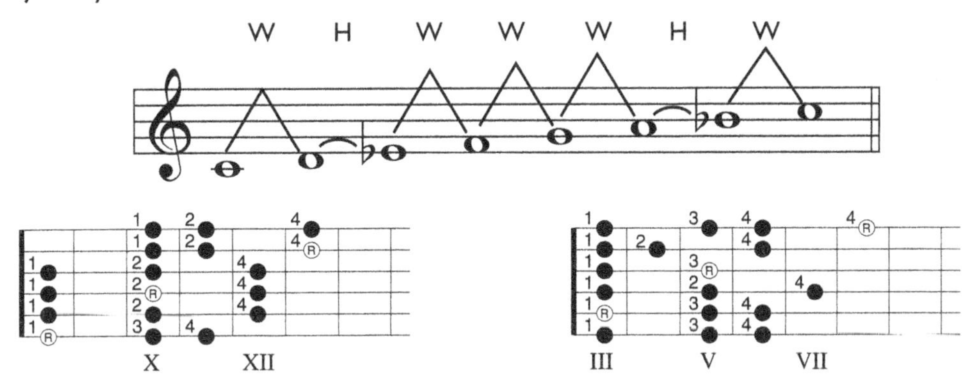

DORIAN ♭2

Use the Dorian ♭2 mode starting on the root of a min11 chord when the 9th is not present and it functions as ii in a minor key.

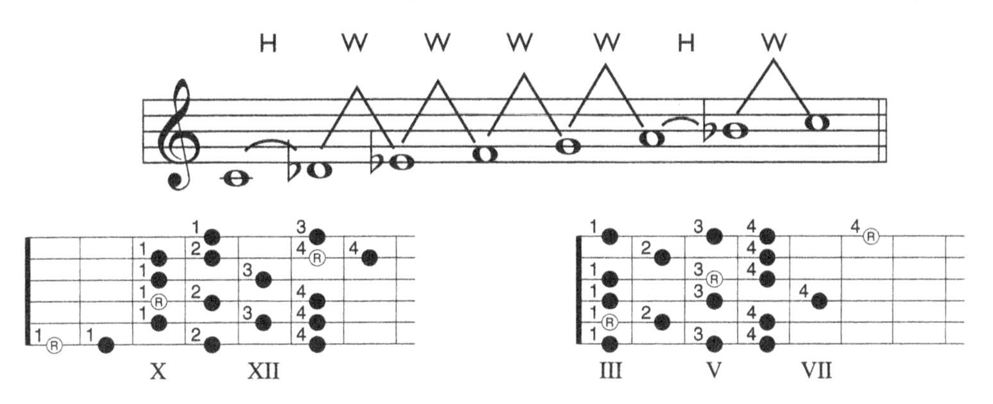

PHRYGIAN

Use the Phrygian mode starting on the root of a min11 chord when the 9th is not present and it functions as iii in a major key.

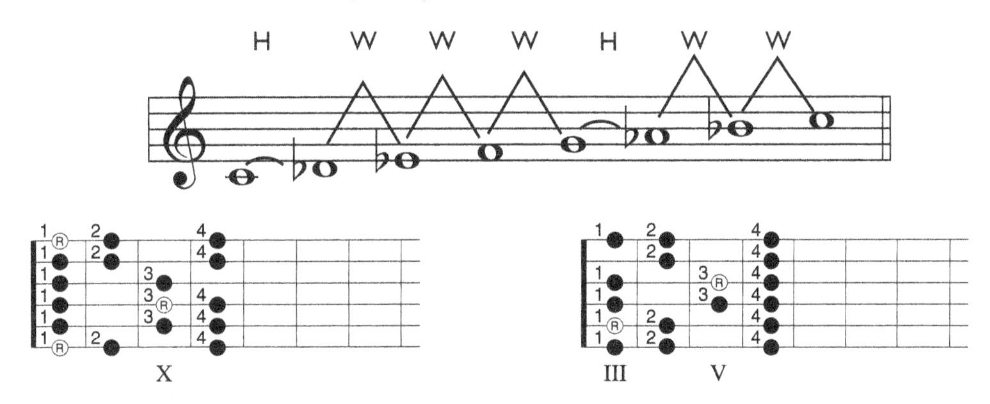

LYDIAN $\flat 3 \flat 7$

Use the Lydian $\flat 3 \flat 7$ mode starting on the root of a min11 chord when it functions as iv in a minor key.

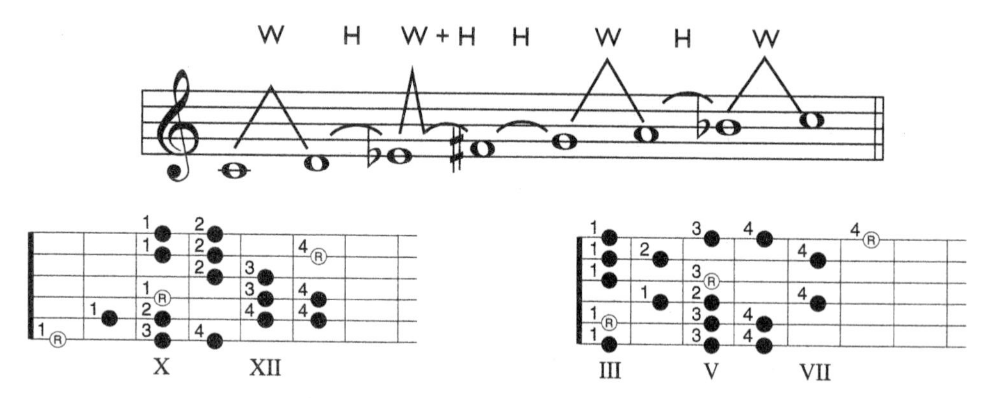

NATURAL MINOR (AEOLIAN)

Use a natural minor scale (Aeolian mode) starting on the root of a min11 chord when it functions as vi in a major key.

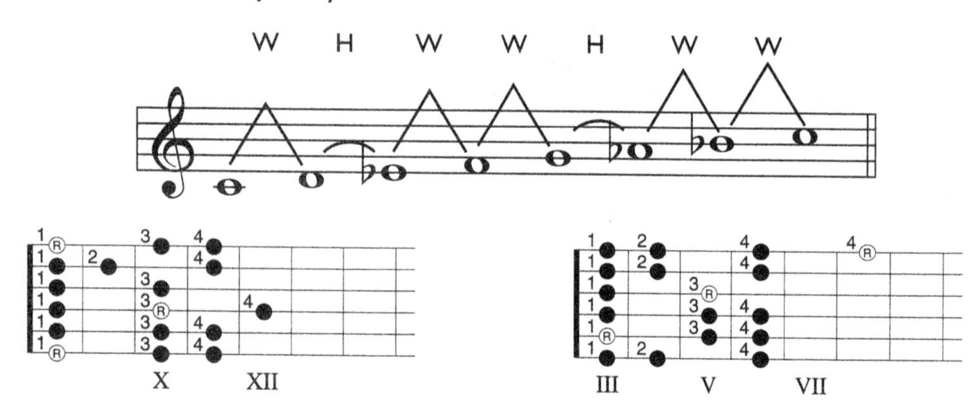

min13 Chords

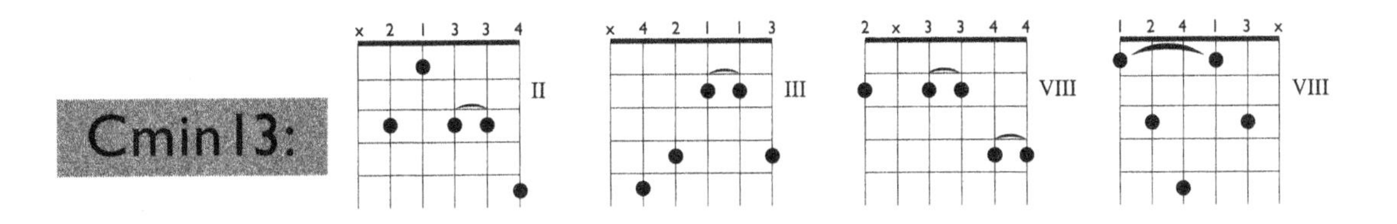

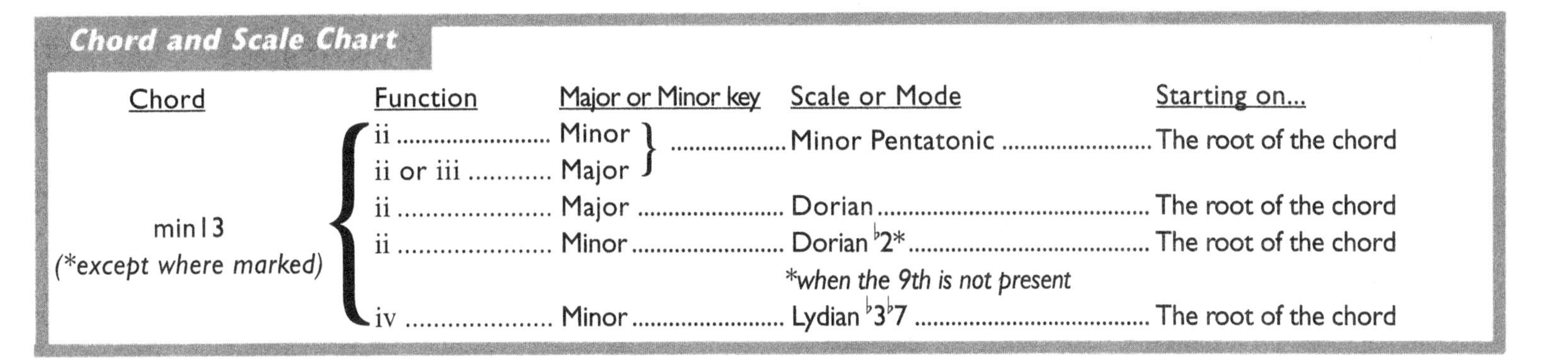

Chord and Scale Chart

Chord	Function	Major or Minor key	Scale or Mode	Starting on...
min13 (*except where marked)	ii	Minor	Minor Pentatonic	The root of the chord
	ii or iii	Major		
	ii	Major	Dorian	The root of the chord
	ii	Minor	Dorian ♭2*	The root of the chord
			*when the 9th is not present	
	iv	Minor	Lydian ♭3♭7	The root of the chord

MINOR PENTATONIC

Use a minor pentatonic scale starting on the root of a min13 chord when it functions as ii in a minor key, or ii or iii in a major key.

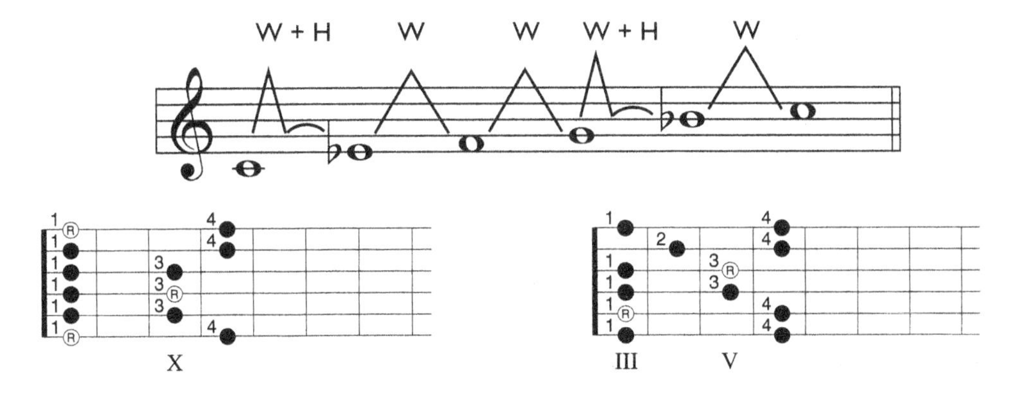

DORIAN

Use the Dorian mode starting on the root of a min13 chord when it functions as ii in a major key.

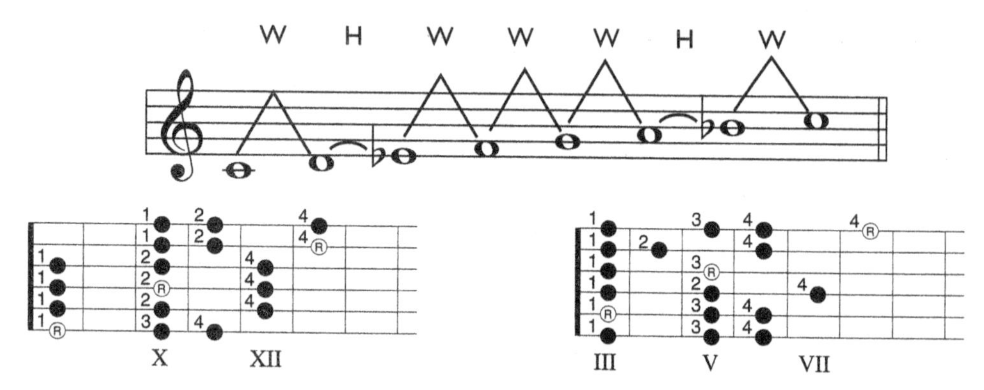

DORIAN ♭2

Use the Dorian ♭2 mode starting on the root of a min13 chord when the 9th is not present and it functions as ii in a minor key.

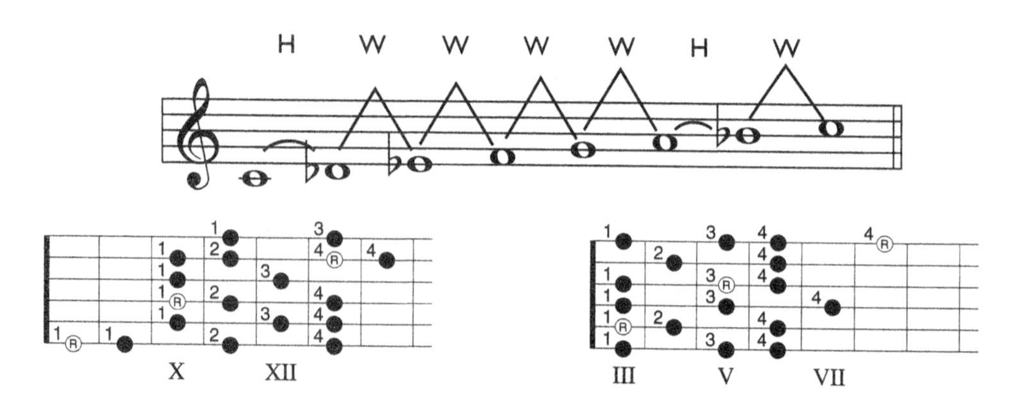

LYDIAN ♭3♭7

Use the Lydian ♭3♭7 mode starting on the root of a min13 chord when it functions as iv in a minor key.

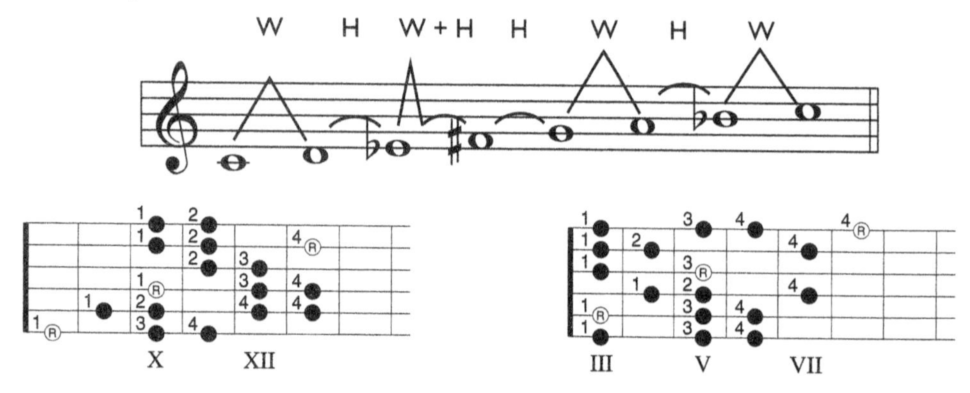

min(Maj7) Chords

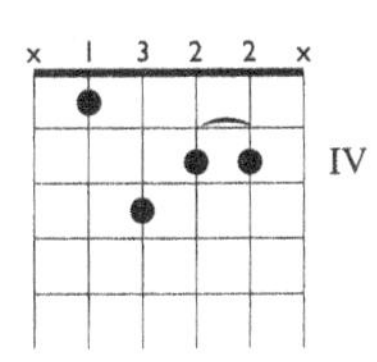

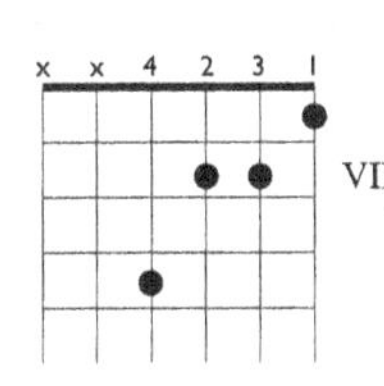

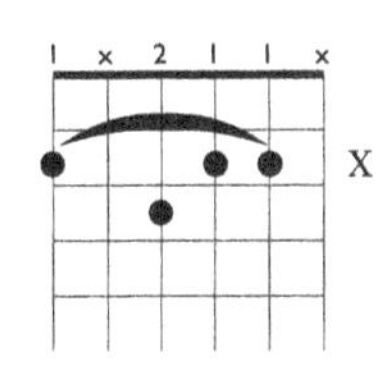

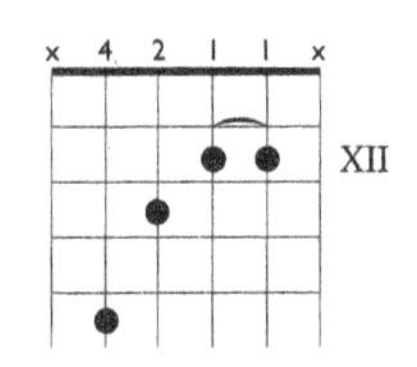

Chord and Scale Chart

Chord	Function	Major or Minor key	Scale or Mode	Starting on...
min(Maj7)	Any	Both	Harmonic Minor	The root of the chord
	Any	Both	Melodic Minor	The root of the chord

HARMONIC MINOR

Use a harmonic minor scale starting on the root of a min(Maj7) chord.

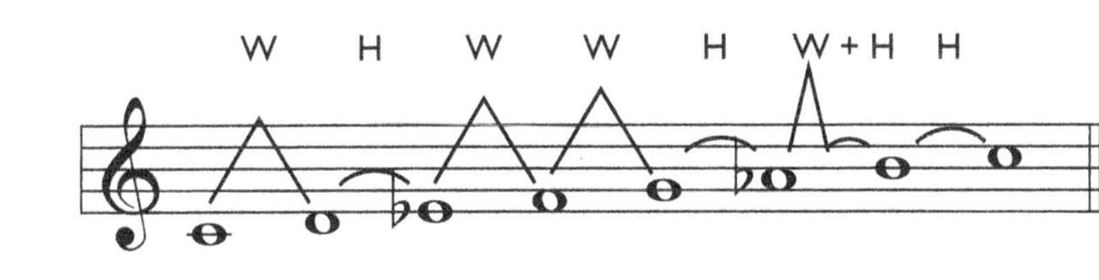

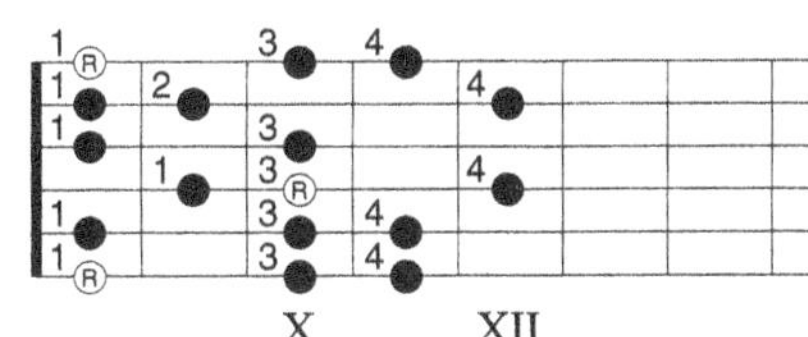

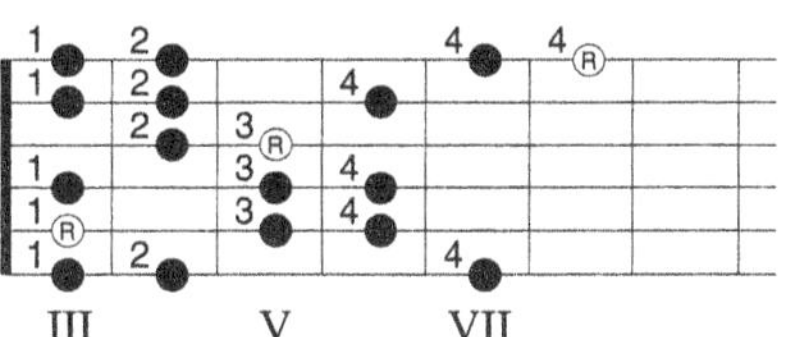

MELODIC MINOR

Use a melodic minor scale starting on the root of a min(Maj7) chord.

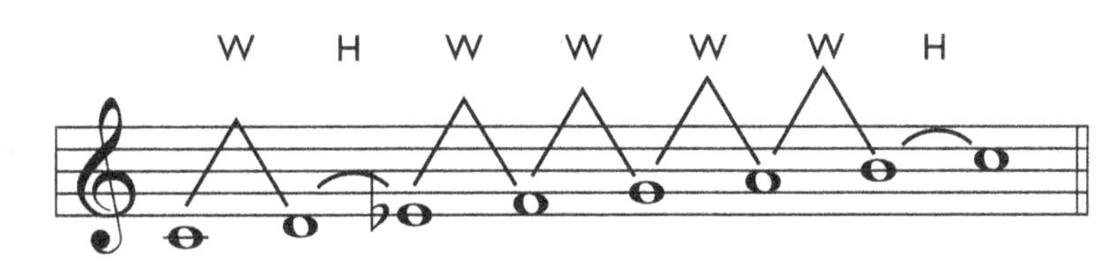

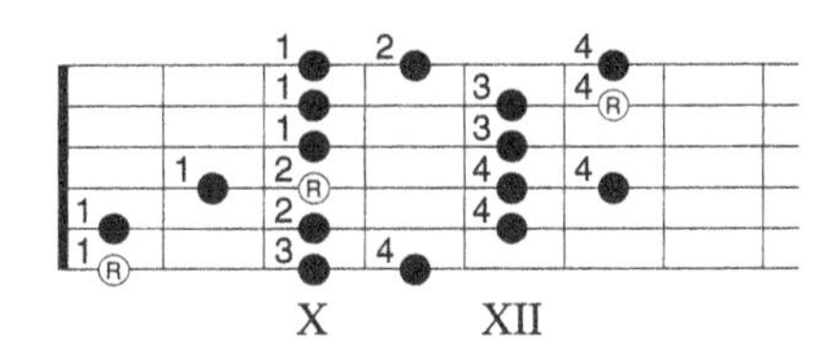

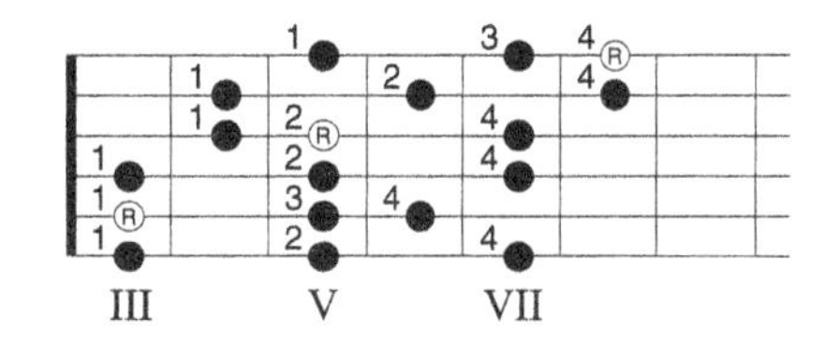

DIMINISHED CHORDS

Diminished, dim7 and min7♭5 (half-diminished) Chords

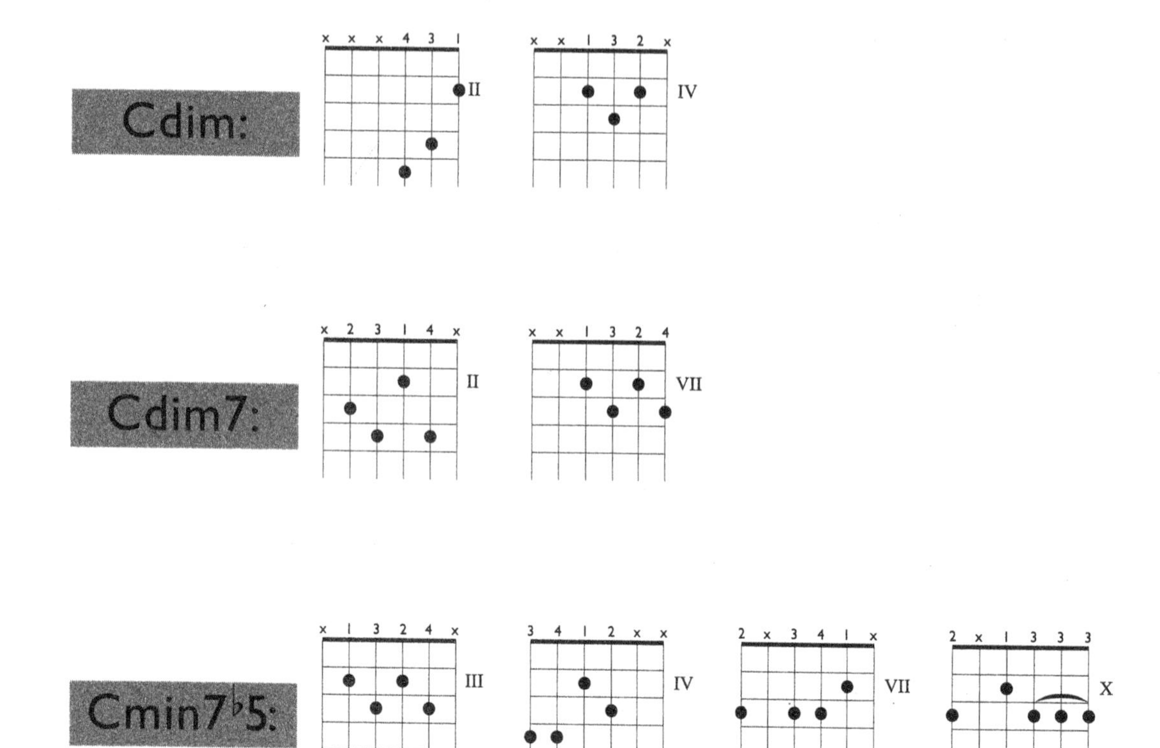

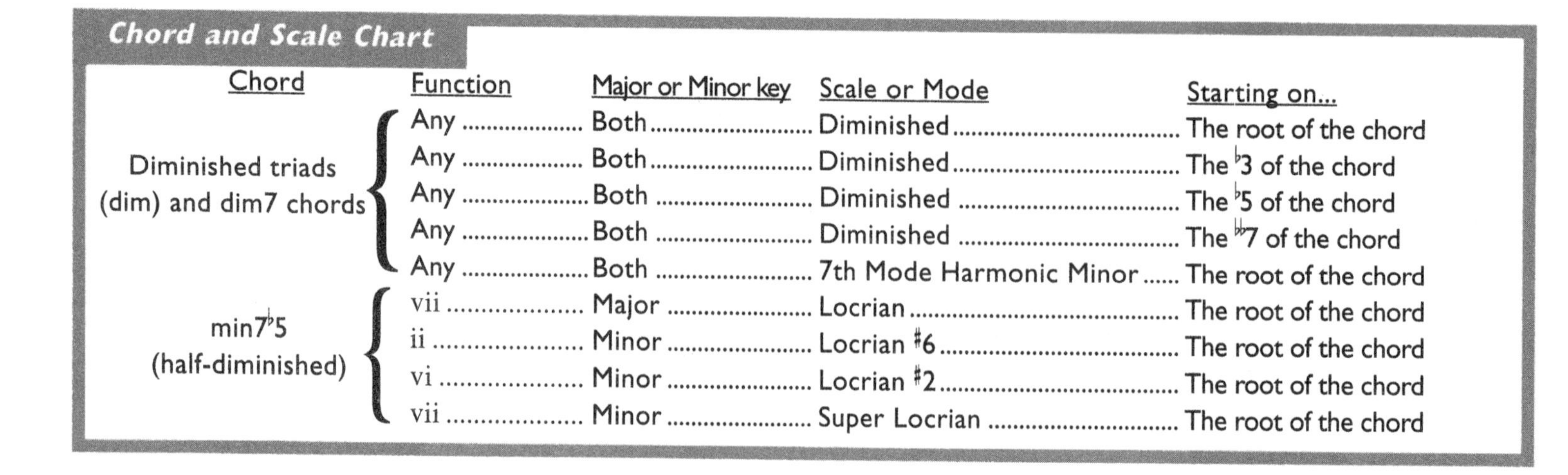

Chord and Scale Chart

Chord	Function	Major or Minor key	Scale or Mode	Starting on...
Diminished triads (dim) and dim7 chords	Any	Both	Diminished	The root of the chord
	Any	Both	Diminished	The ♭3 of the chord
	Any	Both	Diminished	The ♭5 of the chord
	Any	Both	Diminished	The ♭♭7 of the chord
	Any	Both	7th Mode Harmonic Minor	The root of the chord
min7♭5 (half-diminished)	vii	Major	Locrian	The root of the chord
	ii	Minor	Locrian ♯6	The root of the chord
	vi	Minor	Locrian ♯2	The root of the chord
	vii	Minor	Super Locrian	The root of the chord

DIMINISHED

Use a diminished scale starting on the root of a diminished triad or a dim7 chord.

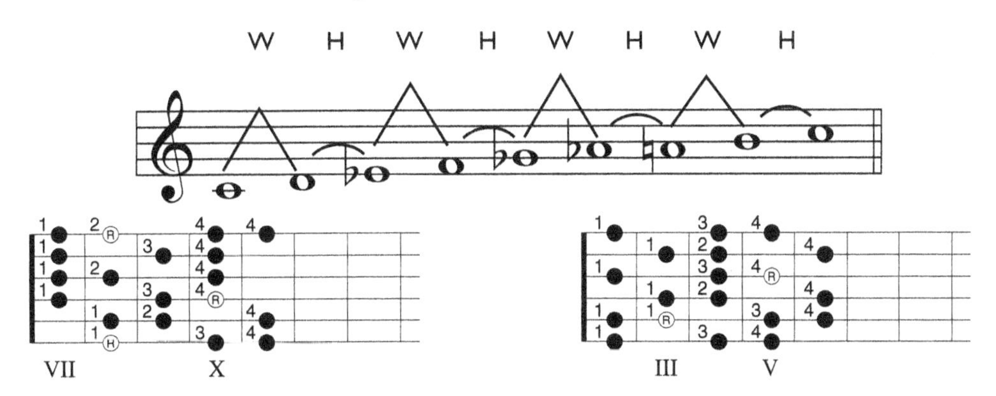

Use a diminished scale starting on the ♭3 of a diminished triad or a dim7 chord.

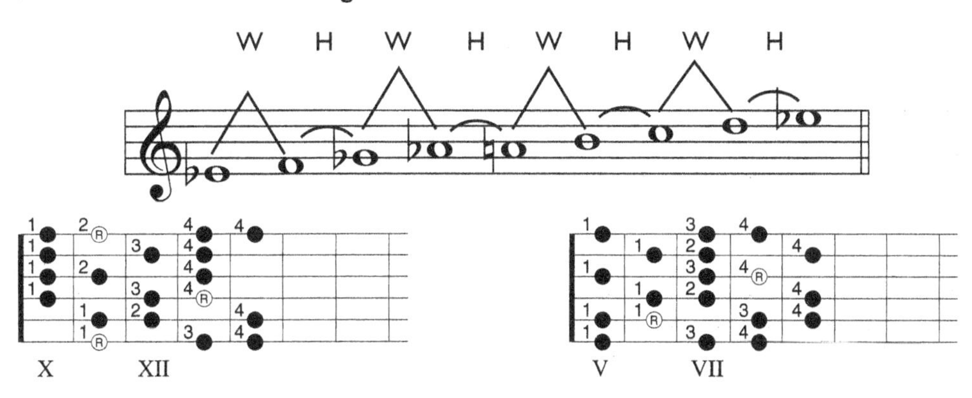

Use a diminished scale starting on the ♭5 of a diminished triad or a dim7 chord.

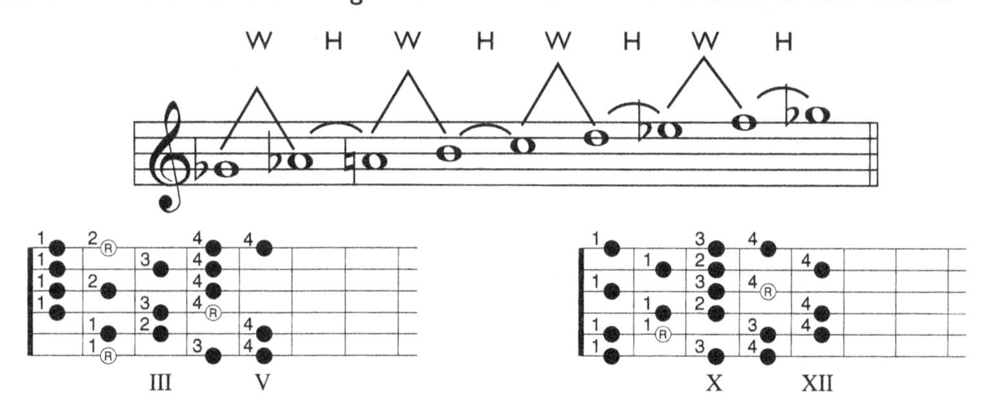

Use a diminished scale starting on the 𝄫7 of a diminished triad or a dim7 chord.

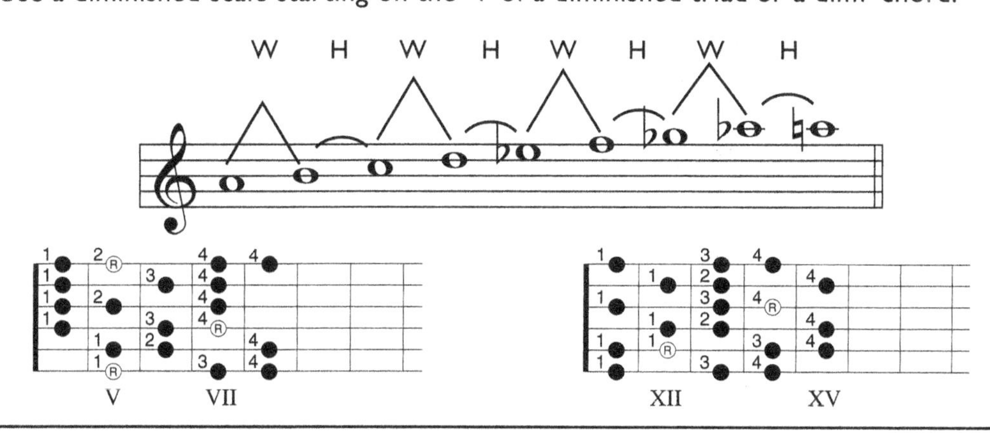

𝄫 = *Double flat.* Lower the note by one whole step (two half steps).

7TH MODE HARMONIC MINOR

Use the 7th mode of the harmonic minor scale starting on the root of a diminished triad or a dim7 chord.

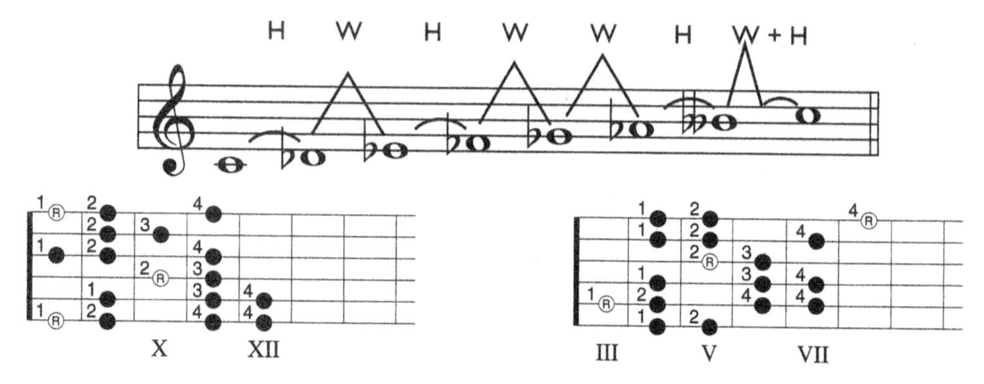

LOCRIAN

Use the Locrian mode starting on the root of a min7♭5 chord when it functions as vii in a major key.

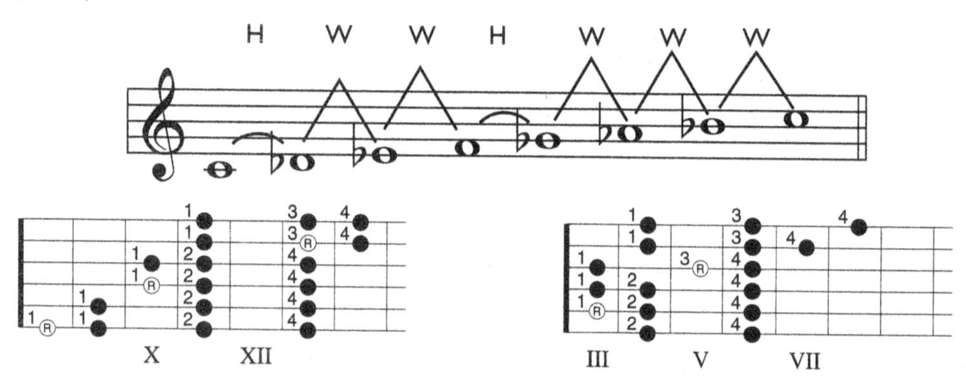

LOCRIAN ♯6

Use the Locrian ♯6 mode starting on the rot of a min7♭5 chord when it functions as ii in a minor key.

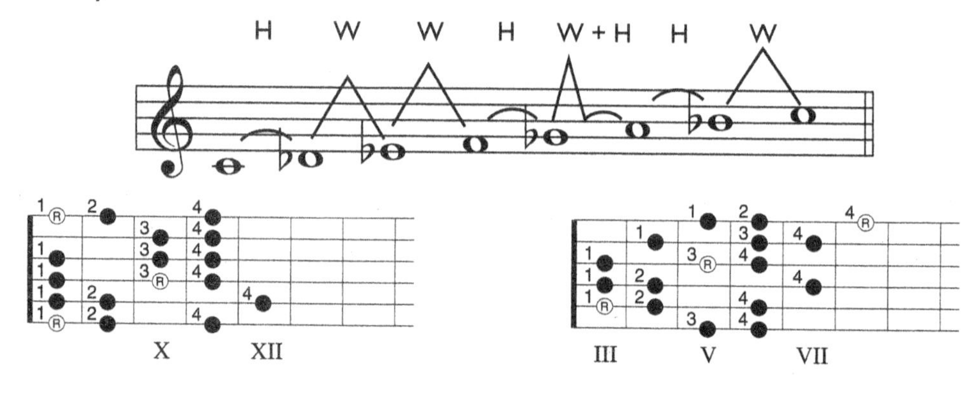

LOCRIAN ♯2

Use the Locrian ♯2 mode starting on the root of a min7♭5 chord when it functions as vi in a minor key.

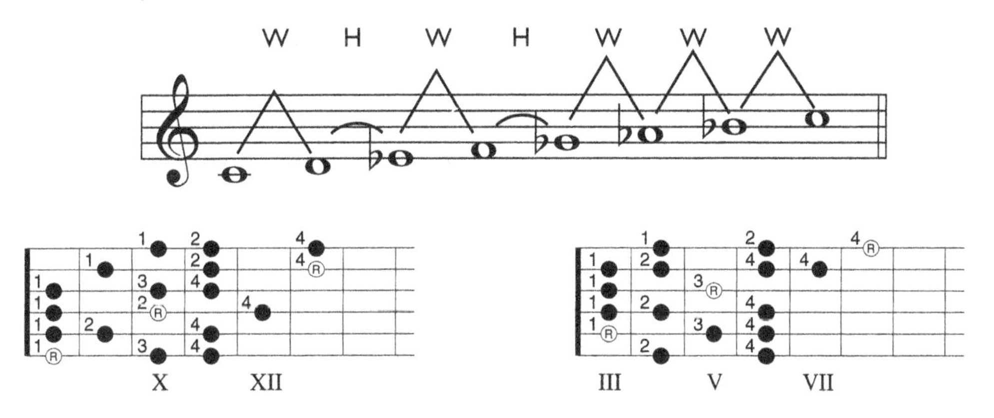

SUPER LOCRIAN

Use the super Locrian mode starting on the root of a min7♭5 chord when it functions as vii in a minor key.

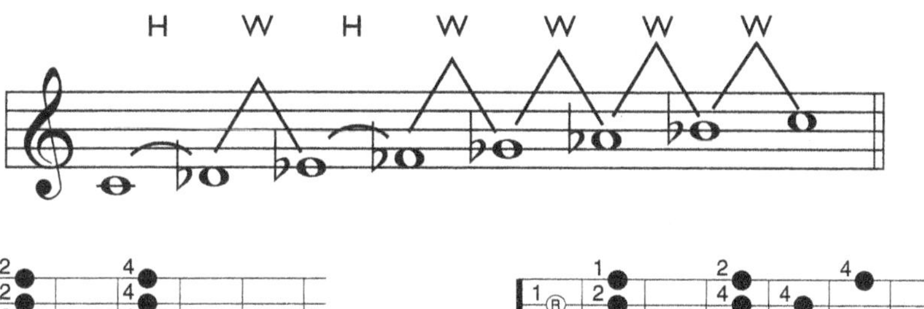

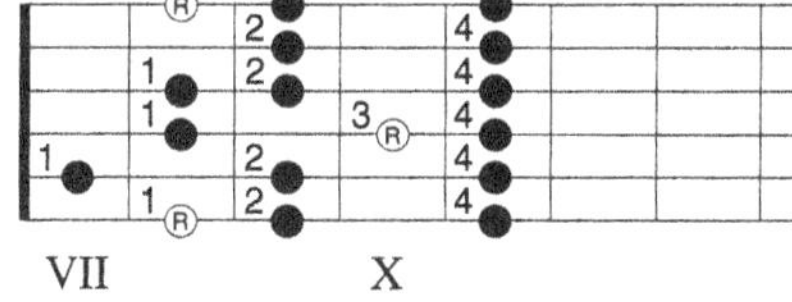

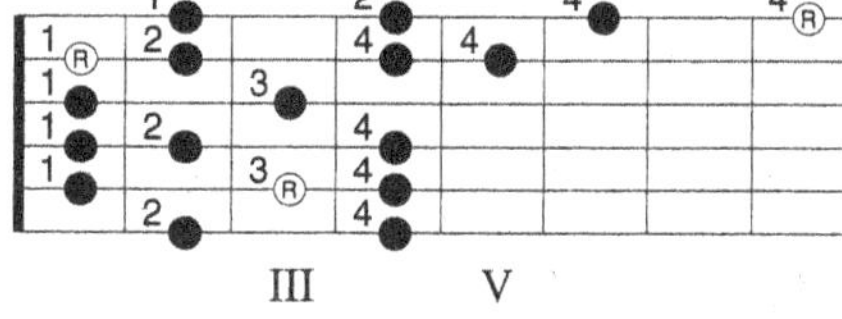

QUARTAL-3 CHORDS

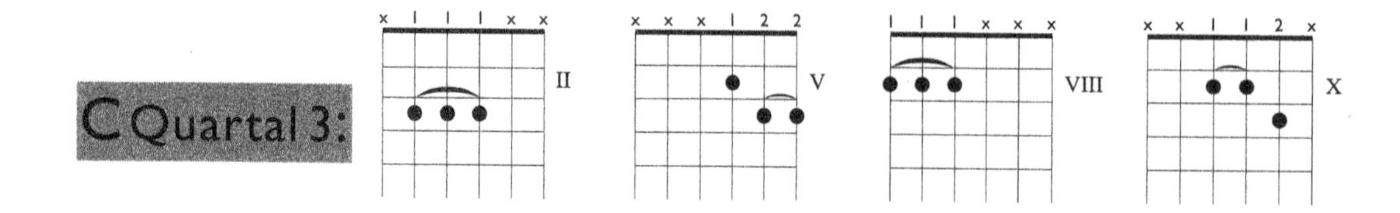

Chord and Scale Chart

Chord	Function	Major or Minor key	Scale or Mode	Starting on...
Quartal-3	Any	Both	Minor Pentatonic	The root of the chord
	Any	Both	Minor Pentatonic	The 4th of the chord
	Any	Both	Minor Pentatonic	The ♭7 of the chord
	Any	Both	Dorian	The root of the chord
	Any	Both	Dorian	The 4th of the chord
	Any	Both	Dorian	The ♭7 of the chord

MINOR PENTATONIC

Use the minor pentatonic scale starting on the root of a quartal-3 chord.

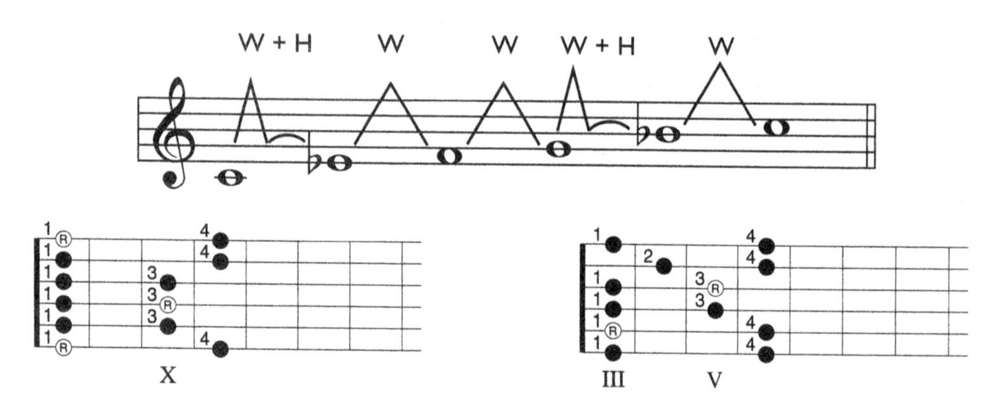

You can also use a minor pentatonic scale starting on the 4th of a quartal-3 chord.

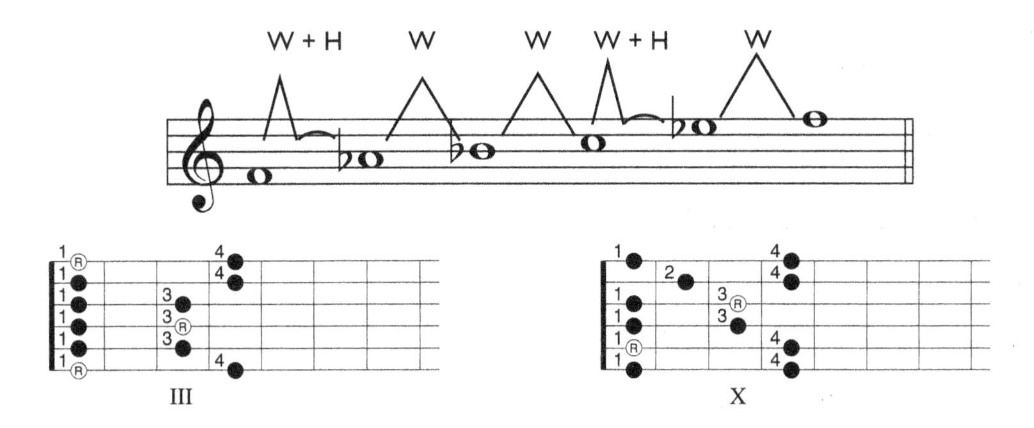

Or, use the minor pentatonic scale starting from the ♭7 of a quartal-3 chord.

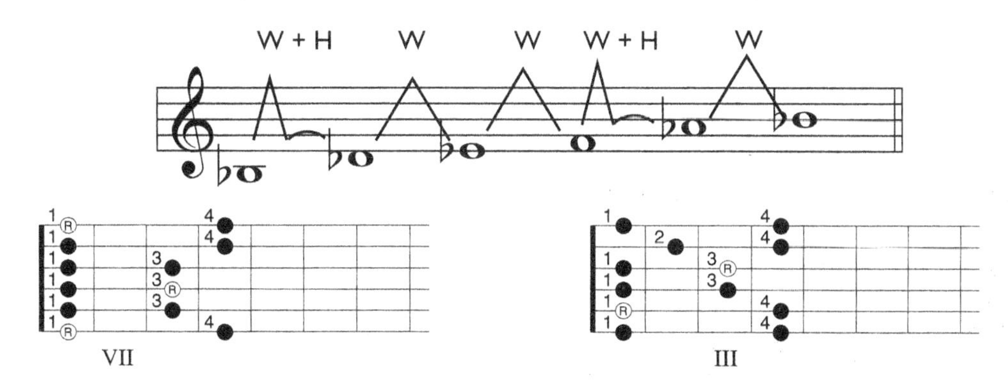

DORIAN

Use the Dorian mode starting from the root of a quartal-3 chord.

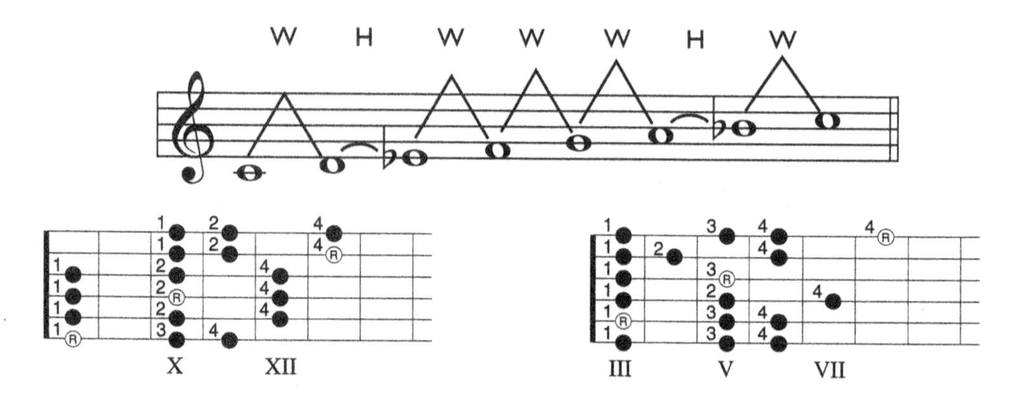

You can also use the Dorian mode starting from the 4th of a quartal-3 chord.

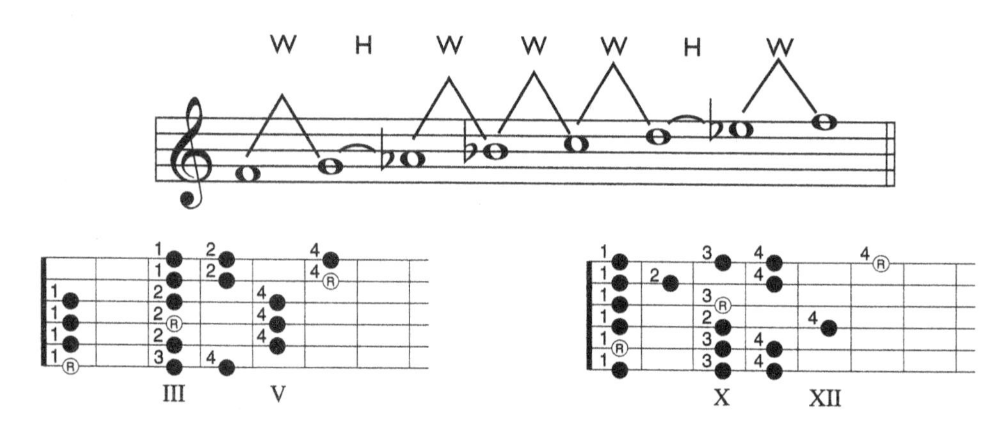

Or, you can use the Dorian mode starting on the ♭7 of a quartal-3 chord.

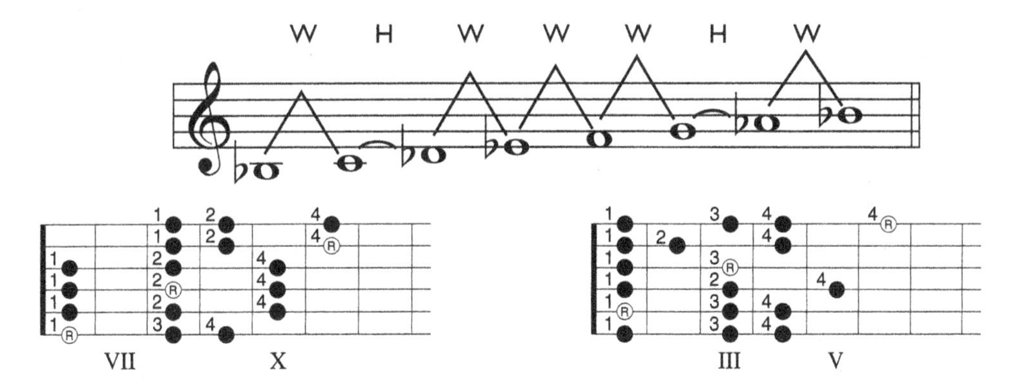

Alfred